The "Trust in British Potatoes"
Recipe Book

Published by the Potato Marketing Board

Potato Marketing Board
50 Hans Crescent, Knightsbridge,
London SW1X 0NB
Telephone: 01-589 4874

D0543086

Contents

Recipes

Front cover photograph taken in The Gallery,
Lanhydrock, near Bodmin.
Pictured from left: Duchesse, Parmentier, Croquette
and Byron Potatoes.

ISBN 0 903623 26 9

Trust in British Potatoes

Your first thoughts on finding a recipe book just about potatoes may well be that it is somewhat unusual and perhaps even that it might be a little boring. But, open the pages, glance at some of the recipes and you will quickly realise that it is the most natural thing in the world to produce a recipe book about the most natural food in the world.

Because that is exactly what potatoes are — a vegetable containing all the necessary nutrients for a healthy diet, low in calories and ready for use in an incredible variety of ways. Potatoes are considered by most people to be an essential part of any meal and represent excellent value for money.

And how appropriate that potatoes, in part symbolising the rich history of British agriculture, should be linked in the pages of this book by an association with the National Trust which is itself vitally concerned with safeguarding an increasing part of Britain's natural and architectural heritage.

So, a warm welcome to this book which sets out to expand and develop your existing interest in, or perhaps even love for, potatoes so that in your future menu planning you need never worry about food looking ordinary — potatoes in so many ways bring meals alive and increase your reputation as a cook.

The Board's London Home Economists pictured in the test kitchen.

At Work with the Potato Marketing Board

The Potato Marketing Board has been in existence since 1934 when it was set up at the request of the potato growers at that time to put a stop to the recurring peaks and troughs in potato production which were such a feature of that era. It is funded chiefly by the potato farmers of Britain, currently numbering about 22,000.

The Board has four main functions, namely:

1 To ensure that annual potato plantings in Great Britain are sufficient to meet the country's requirements.

2 To set and enforce a quality standard for British potatoes.

3 To sponsor research into all aspects of the production and marketing of the crop.

4 To promote greater interest in, and awareness and consumption of, British potatoes.

The home economists employed by the Board, currently four, are responsible for the operation of test and experimental kitchens in London and Edinburgh which perform a variety of functions. First and foremost amongst these is the development and testing of potato recipes for use in leaflets, booklets and of course this recipe book. The home economics section has nearly 1,000 potato recipes on its files covering a range of dishes from soups to cakes and so is never at a loss to produce something exciting for that special occasion.

Then there are the cookery demonstrations; approximately 1,500 undertaken every year by a 50-strong team throughout the country who visit local groups to present an evening of potato cookery which includes a quiz with prizes. On the more specialist front demonstrations are also presented to schools and catering establishments. See page 93 for details.

A range of leaflets are produced which not only cover potato cookery in general terms but also the specialist requirements of those interested in microwave cookery, freezing, and other food techniques. For everyone there is the potato variety chart — a comprehensive assessment of the various attributes of the chief potato varieties likely to be found in the shops during the year.

During the summer months home economists from the Board attend many of the principal outdoor shows and events to present cookery demonstrations and deal with enquiries from visitors.

Below Stairs with the National Trust

A visit to many a National Trust historic home today will highlight the importance of cooking — as well as eating — in shaping our architectural heritage. For it is often not just the sumptuous dining rooms of grand mansions which are now on show, but also their vast "below stairs" areas and the family kitchens of cottages or farmhouses.

Take the stone-flagged kitchen of *East Riddlesden Hall*, a seventeenth century Yorkshire manor house, or that of the tiny timber-framed *Oakhurst Cottage*, near Godalming in Surrey, which can only take six visitors at a time, strictly by appointment.

In complete contrast are the Victorian kitchen and other fascinating "below stairs" rooms at *Uppark*. Built in 1690, high on the Sussex Downs, the house was re-decorated and furnished in the mid-eighteenth century. One of the nineteenth century changes was the replacement of the detached kitchen by a new, more convenient one, in the basement of the house itself.

At *Cotehele* in Cornwall, where a Kitchen Court lies in the centre of the medieval house, the changes have gone on around a kitchen which pre-dates the arrival of the potato in Britain. Although conveniently sited in the days when the household ate in the Hall, it was less well

placed when customs changed and the family created its first dining room. But when the east wing was reconstructed in 1862 a second dining room was built, this time next door to the kitchen.

Today's guests at *Cotehele* can sample traditional West Country dishes in the restored barn which now houses a National Trust restaurant. For, as well as caring for historic buildings and over half a million acres of countryside, the Trust has a considerable reputation for catering. It owns and manages some 90 restaurants, cafes, tearooms and kiosks, and also two small inns.

Proceeds from these help the Trust maintain all the places of historic interest or natural beauty entrusted to its care in England, Wales and Northern Ireland. There is also a sister organisation, The National Trust for Scotland, doing the same excellent work north of the border.

As independent charities they rely heavily on the subscriptions of their members who are entitled to free admission to an ever growing list of properties. For more details see page 96.

The two National Trusts are very pleased to be associated with this Potato Marketing Board recipe book

In the kitchen of Victorian industrialist and scientific genius, Lord Armstrong, at Cragside, Northumberland, a service lift connects with the scullery in the basement.

History of the British Potato

History is quite clear about the origins of the potato — the Incas grew them for hundreds of years in the foothills of the Andes, in Peru, South America — but is less clear on when and how it first came to Europe. Depending on which history book you read Hawkins, Raleigh and Drake are all credited with introducing the potato to Britain but whichever of these well-known gentlemen was responsible we can safely assume that potatoes travelled as ships stores and as a result were subsequently accredited, quite rightly, with being responsible for the elimination of scurvy — the disease which so afflicted seamen in those days due to the lack of Vitamin C in their diet.

At first the potato was treated with some suspicion and it was only when Louis XVI of France began wearing potato flowers in his buttonhole that it became a popular vegetable. Too popular in some respects because the virtual dependence on the potato crop by the people of Ireland brought starvation and death when the crop failed in two successive years (1845, 1846) due to blight. As a result of this disaster many of those who survived emigrated to North America resulting in the largest single population loss ever experienced by any country and without doubt changing the course of history.

On the streets of London and other big cities in Victorian times the baked potato man was a common sight.
He would call:

"Here's taters hot, my little chaps,
Now just lay out a copper,
I'm known all up and down the Strand,
You won't find any hotter"

Children in particular would run to buy his wares on cold days and gentlemen would purchase potatoes for their ladies to hold in their muffs to keep their hands warm.

Nowadays of course modern farming methods ensure that the potato crop is not seriously affected by the ravages of weather or disease and that adequate supplies are available at all times to feed the nation.

Nutritional Value of British Potatoes

With the greater awareness of, and interest in, healthy eating the nutrient value of the potato is now very much appreciated. With its contribution of Vitamin C, Vitamin B6, Calcium, Copper and Fibre to the diet it is hardly surprising that potato consumption in Britain is rising to a higher level than any other European country. And because potatoes are so versatile they can be used in soups, snacks, composite meals, even desserts. For those of you who like to keep an eye on your waistline there is more good news; for instance potatoes are very low in calories — just 23 calories per ounce for plain boiled.

The table below shows interesting comparisons — which may surprise you!

Potatoes are not fattening if eaten in moderation and cooked without fat. Potatoes boiled or baked in their jackets can be an especially tasty and useful addition to a calorie controlled diet.

Chemical / nutrient composition of the raw potato

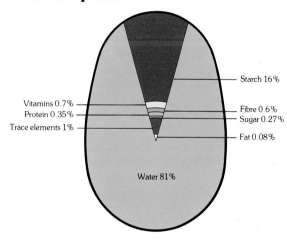

Starch 16%
Fibre 0.6%
Sugar 0.27%
Fat 0.08%
Vitamins 0.7%
Protein 0.35%
Trace elements 1%
Water 81%

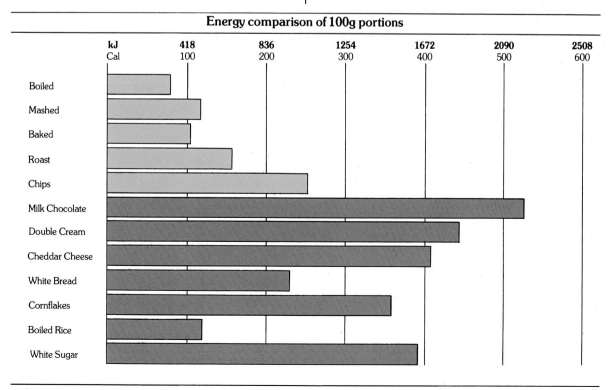

Energy comparison of 100g portions

	kJ / Cal	418 / 100	836 / 200	1254 / 300	1672 / 400	2090 / 500	2508 / 600
Boiled							
Mashed							
Baked							
Roast							
Chips							
Milk Chocolate							
Double Cream							
Cheddar Cheese							
White Bread							
Cornflakes							
Boiled Rice							
White Sugar							

Varieties of British Potatoes

There are several hundred different varieties of potato grown throughout the world and over 50 of these are grown in Britain. However, more than 90% of our total production is accounted for by just nine maincrop and six early varieties.

The guide below provides useful information on these 15 varieties which are most frequently available to you. Use it to provide an indication of when to expect them in your shops. As it is now law that the variety name must be clearly shown it is much easier for you to be selective and choose those which best suit your family.

	June	July	August	September	October	November	December	January	February	March	April	May

Home Guard — Usually the first 'new' potato. More floury than other early varieties.

Wilja — This potato is long and oval in shape with a yellow flesh. It cooks particularly well, especially when boiled.

Arran Comet — Mainly Kent grown, these cream-fleshed potatoes are available early in the season.

Estima — A yellow-fleshed potato which cooks extremely well and, like Wilja, is ideal for boiling.

Ulster Sceptre — A very reliable potato of good cooking quality which is long oval in shape and has a white skin and flesh.

Désirée — A red-skinned potato with yellow flesh. An excellent all-round potato but particularly good when boiled, baked or chipped.

Maris Bard — An oval-shaped potato with good cooking quality.

Maris Piper — The most popular maincrop variety. Potatoes are attractive and suitable for most cooking uses.

Pentland Javelin — The most widely-grown early potato. Attractive looking potatoes with good cooking quality.

Cara — These potatoes are large and round and are particularly good for baking. They are parti-coloured with a white skin and pink eyes.

Epicure — Grown in South-West Scotland they have a distinctive appearance and flavour.

Pentland Crown — A popular variety whose flesh tends to be less floury than other maincrop varieties.

King Edward — This potato was named after King Edward VII and is still the most widely-known variety. The flesh is very floury which makes it ideal for mashing or roasting.

Pentland Squire — A potato with a very white skin and flesh. Has particularly good cooking qualities especially when baked.

Romano — Another red-skinned variety similar to Désirée both in appearance and cooking suitability.

Illustrated above is a selection of varieties
of British maincrop potatoes.

Your Assurance of Quality with British Potatoes

To ensure that consumers can be confident of buying potatoes which are of a satisfactory quality, the Potato Marketing Board sets a standard — known as the Ware Standard — to which all potatoes sold to the public must comply. The standard provides for the exclusion of potatoes which are:

<u>Shrivelled or wizened</u>

<u>Damaged</u> beyond redress by peeling to a maximum of 3mm

<u>Diseased</u> or affected by rots

Covered by <u>common scab</u> over more than 25% of the surface

Affected by <u>greening</u>

<u>Bruised or discoloured</u> internally

Damaged by <u>wireworm</u>, slugs or other <u>pests</u>

Damaged by <u>frost</u>

<u>Mis-shapen</u> or affected by <u>growth cracks</u>, <u>second</u> <u>growth</u> or <u>hollow heart</u>

<u>Tainted</u>

Affected by <u>growth shoots</u>

Most potatoes purchased will fall within a size band of 45mm — 85mm but potatoes measuring below or above these sizes can be sold as small or large respectively provided they also comply with the Standard in terms of the exclusions mentioned above.

It is not generally appreciated that potatoes are fragile and bruise easily and that therefore they should be treated gently. In fact it is no exaggeration to suggest that they should be handled like eggs. This careful handling should extend throughout the life of the potato from harvesting to cooking to ensure that neither skin damage nor internal bruising occur. Light, whether natural or artificial is one of the chief enemies of the potato as prolonged exposure will cause the potato to turn green and taste bitter.

Of course the Potato Marketing Board's strict quality standard should ensure that no greening has occurred before you purchase the potatoes but remember that daylight or artificial light in your home will have the same affect so always store your potatoes in the dark and in a cool dry place to avoid any tendency for them to sprout or rot which can occur in warm humid conditions.

A select sample of size graded (45-85mm) potatoes.

Microwave Cookery with British Potatoes

Microwave ovens are ideal for fast, economical cooking, but for those of you more used to conventional cookers, it may take a while to become familiar with them. Here is some useful information to help you make the most of British potatoes in your microwave oven.

When boiling potatoes, a small amount of water is sufficient, although when cooking larger quantities a little extra water will ensure even cooking.

Cut the potato into even-sized pieces, whether sliced, diced or whole, and stir once or twice during cooking. This will also ensure even cooking.

Rinse the prepared potatoes in cold water to remove excess starch and to prevent them from becoming sticky when cooked.

A small amount of lemon juice added before cooking will prevent the potatoes from blackening.

Unless stated otherwise, cover potatoes when boiling to trap the steam, apart from when baking potatoes.

Small quantities of potatoes up to 1lb (450g) will cook more evenly than large quantities.

Leave the potatoes to stand for a few minutes after their cooking time to allow cooking to finish.

Do not try any deep or shallow frying — microwave ovens have no temperature control so that fats could easily get overheated.

A browning dish is used fairly successfully with oven chips as it helps to turn them slightly crisp. They can be cooked straight from the freezer on the maximum setting. Place 8oz (225g) of the chips in the oven, uncovered, cook for 2 minutes, stir, then cook for a further 2 minutes. It also cooks croquettes satisfactorily as long as they have been defrosted. Eight frozen potato croquettes weighing 1oz (25g) each can be defrosted and reheated in four minutes by using the maximum heat setting and turning once. *Do not cover.* However, not all frozen potato products can be cooked in a browning dish.

When using a turntable, remember to put larger items around the outside edge to make the cooking more efficient.

Roast potatoes, sauté and chips can be cooked conventionally and reheated in the microwave oven although they will not remain crisp. As a general rule 1lb (450g) of cooked potatoes will take 2 minutes to reheat.

For mashed potatoes simply cook the potatoes in the microwave, drain, mash and return to the microwave for 1 minute on maximum.

Where cooked potatoes are to be used for salads, it is a good idea to rinse them in cold water.

The booklet illustrated contains additional useful information as well as recipes adapted for microwave cooking. It is available on request from:

The Potato Marketing Board
50 Hans Crescent, Knightsbridge, London SW1X 0NB
Telephone: 01-589 4874

Power Ratings

Microwave ovens have different power ratings, so that cooking times will vary. Opposite is a table which explains the adjustment you will need to make in calculating your cooking times.

Wattage of oven	Cooking Time (minutes)
500	12-13
650	10
700	8-9

Jacket Potatoes

Opposite is a table to enable you to calculate the correct cooking times, using the maximum setting on your oven.

The skins of the potatoes should be pricked prior to cooking. Remember to turn them half way through their cooking time, and bear in mind that times do vary with the potatoes and oven used.

Quantity	Size	Cooking Time (minutes) 650 watt oven
1	12oz (350g)	9
1	10oz (275g)	7
1	8oz (225g)	6
2	8oz (225g)	12
3	8oz (225g)	17
4	8oz (225g)	20

Cooking Potatoes in the Microwave

Preparation	Quantity	Water	Cooking Time (minutes) 650 watt oven
Cut into 2oz (50g) pieces to be partially cooked (i.e. for roasting).	1lb (450g)	2 tblspn 2 × 15ml spn	5 minutes stir once
	2lb (900g)	3 tblspn 3 × 15ml spn	8 minutes stir once
Cut into 2oz (50g) pieces to be fully cooked.	1lb (450g)	2 tblspn 2 × 15ml spn	10 minutes stir once
	2lb (900g)	3 tblspn 3 × 15ml spn	14 minutes stir once
Cut into ¼" (7mm) thick slices to be partially cooked (i.e. layered dishes, toppings, sauté).	1lb (450g)	2 tblspn 2 × 15ml spn	5 minutes stir once
	2lb (900g)	3 tblspn 3 × 15ml spn	8 minutes stir once
Cut into ¼" (7mm) thick slices to be fully cooked.	1lb (450g)	2 tblspn 2 × 15ml spn	8 minutes stir once
	2lb (900g)	3 tblspn 3 × 15ml spn	14 minutes stir once
Cut into ½" (15mm) dice, to be fully cooked.	1lb (450g)	2 tblspn 2 × 15ml spn	8 minutes stir twice stand for 5 minutes
	2lb (900g)	3 tblspn 3 × 15ml spn	12 minutes stir twice stand for 5 minutes

Soups and Starters

There is nothing new about making soups with potatoes. That idea has been with us for many years but was probably never put to greater use than during the early years of the century when the combination of poverty and poor health care caused the working population to recognise the potato as a double salvation — it was highly nutritious and therefore aided good health and was cheap, so even those on the lowest incomes could afford it. Today, happily the reasons for making potato soup are slightly different. In a world which is encouraged, more than ever before, to eat healthily but economically, what better way of achieving those two goals than by using potatoes to form the basis for a range of soups which will give everyone a glow — inside and out! In this chapter you will find a wide range of recipe ideas including Highland Prawns — a special treat for everyone who enjoys shellfish; and don't forget your cooked soup can be safely kept in your freezer for up to three months.

One of the original fireplaces in the Tudor Merchant's House at Tenby, Pembrokeshire.

Pots and pans at the ready in the kitchen of Castle Drogo, Devon, built 1910 to 1930.

"The Spur in the Dish" by Bell Scott at Wallington, Northumberland, illustrates an old border custom.

17

Pictured from left:
North Sea Scallops, Country Mushroom Paté,
Breton Fish Soup, Potato and Asparagus Soup,
Ham Salad Rolls.

Country Mushroom Paté

Ingredients

1½oz	butter	40g
4oz	bacon, de-rinded and chopped	125g
1 medium	onion, chopped	1 medium
4oz	mushrooms, chopped	125g
1 clove	garlic, crushed	1 clove
1lb	chicken livers	450g
2 tblspn	brandy	2 × 15ml spn
1 tspn	thyme	1 × 5ml spn
1 tspn	lemon juice	1 × 5ml spn
	salt and black pepper	
1lb	British potatoes, cooked and sieved	450g

Method

1 **Melt** the butter and gently fry the bacon, onion, mushrooms, garlic and the chicken livers until cooked.
2 **Stir** in the brandy, thyme, lemon juice, salt and black pepper and fry for a further 3-4 minutes.
3 **Liquidise** or place in a food processor with the potato and purée the mixture.
4 **Place** the mixture in a 2lb (900g) loaf tin or 2pt (1.2ltr) soufflé dish and leave to chill.

Potato and Asparagus Soup

Ingredients — Serves 4

1oz	butter	25g
1lb	British potatoes, diced	450g
1	onion, chopped	1
10oz	broccoli, chopped	275g
1pt	chicken stock	600ml
2 × 12oz cans	asparagus	2 × 350g cans
	salt and black pepper	

Garnish: parsley, chopped

Method

1 **Melt** the butter in a large saucepan, add the potatoes, onion and broccoli. Cook for 5 minutes.
2 **Add** the stock and asparagus and simmer for 20 minutes.
3 **Season** and allow to cool.
4 **Purée** the soup in a blender or sieve and re-heat.
5 **Serve** with chopped parsley.

Curried Parsnip Soup

Ingredients — Serves 4

1	onion, sliced	1
8oz	parsnips, sliced	225g
8oz	British potatoes, sliced	225g
1 clove	garlic, crushed	1 clove
2oz	butter	50g
1oz	flour	25g
2 tspn	mild curry powder	2 × 5ml spn
2pt	stock	1 litre
	salt and black pepper	

Garnish: single cream

Method

1 **In** a deep saucepan sauté the vegetables in the butter for 10 minutes.
2 **Stir** in the flour and curry powder and continue cooking for 2-3 minutes.
3 **Pour** in the stock, season to taste and bring to the boil.
Cover and simmer gently for 20 minutes.
4 **Liquidise** or sieve the soup, check the seasoning and reheat. Serve garnished with swirls of cream.

Tomato and Orange Soup

Ingredients — Serves 4

1 large	onion, chopped	1 large
1 large	carrot, grated	1 large
1oz	butter	25g
15oz can	chopped tomatoes	400g can
8oz	British potatoes, sliced thinly	225g
1 tspn	mixed herbs	1 × 5ml spn
½ tspn	demerara sugar	1 × 2.5ml spn
1	orange, rind and juice	1
1pt	chicken stock	600ml
	salt and black pepper	
¼pt	single cream	150ml

Garnish: parsley

Method

1 **In** a deep saucepan fry the onion and carrot gently in butter until soft.
2 **Add** all the other ingredients except the cream and simmer gently for 30 minutes.
3 **Liquidise** the soup or pass through a sieve.
4 **Add** the cream, adjust the seasoning and reheat but do **not** boil.
5 **Serve** garnished with a sprig of parsley.

19

Pictured from left:
Country Mushroom Paté, Curried Parsnip Soup, Potato and
Asparagus Soup, Tomato and Orange Soup.

Pictured from left:
Potato and Watercress Soup, Breton Fish Soup, Potato and
Chicken Soup.

Potato and Watercress Soup

Ingredients		Serves 4
1	onion, chopped	1
1oz	butter	25g
1 tblspn	oil	1 × 15ml spn
2 bunches	watercress, chopped	2 bunches
1lb	British potatoes, diced	450g
1pt	chicken stock	600ml
	salt and black pepper	
¼pt	milk	150ml

Method

1 **Fry** the onion in the butter and oil until soft. Add the watercress and potatoes and fry for a further minute.

2 **Pour** in the stock followed by the seasoning, bring to the boil and simmer for 30 minutes.

3 **Remove** from the heat and cool, then sieve or liquidise and return to the saucepan.

4 **Add** the milk, reheat and serve hot.

Breton Fish Soup

Ingredients		Serves 4
2 sticks	celery, finely sliced	2 sticks
4oz	carrots, roughly grated	125g
1 clove	garlic, crushed	1 clove
8oz	British potatoes, diced	225g
¾pt	chicken stock	450ml
	salt and pepper	
12oz	white fish, cubed	350g
1 tblspn	cornflour	1 × 15ml spn
¼pt	milk	150ml
2 tblspn	parsley, chopped	2 × 15ml spn

Method

1 **Put** the vegetables into a saucepan with the chicken stock and seasoning. Bring to the boil, then simmer gently for 20 minutes.

2 **Add** the fish and continue to simmer for a further 10 minutes.

3 **Add** a little of the milk to the cornflour and add to the soup.

4 **Pour** in the remainder of the milk, add parsley. Reheat the soup, adjust seasoning and serve.

N.B. This soup is virtually a meal in itself.

Potato and Chicken Soup

Ingredients		Serves 4
1lb	British potatoes, diced	450g
1 large	onion, chopped	1 large
3 sticks	celery, chopped	3 sticks
1oz	butter	25g
1½pt	chicken stock	900ml
1	bay leaf	1
	salt and black pepper	
8oz	chicken, cooked and finely chopped	225g
Garnish: parsley, chopped		

Method

1 **Fry** the potatoes, onion and celery in the butter in a large saucepan for 5 minutes.

2 **Pour** in the stock, add the bay leaf and seasoning. Bring to the boil. Cover and simmer for 20 minutes.

3 **Allow** to cool, then sieve or liquidise the soup.

4 **Return** to the saucepan and stir in the chicken, season to taste and bring to the boil. Simmer for 5 minutes. Remove bay leaf.

5 **Serve** garnished with chopped parsley.

High windows light great wooden rafters above one of the grandest kitchens in Britain at Lanhydrock, near Bodmin.

Smoked Mackerel Paté

Ingredients

4oz	smoked mackerel fillets	125g
8oz	British potatoes, cooked and sieved	225g
3oz	cream cheese	75g
¼pt	single cream	150ml
1 tblspn	lemon juice	1 × 15ml spn
2 tblspn	brandy	2 × 15ml spn

Method

1 **Remove** skin from the mackerel fillets and flake the fish.

2 **Place** all the ingredients into a food processor or blender and blend until smooth

3 **Place** in 1 large or 8 individual serving dishes and chill well.

4 **Serve** with crusty bread.

Highland Prawns

Ingredients
Serves 4

1 small	onion, chopped	1 small
1oz	butter	25g
6oz	British new potatoes, or small maincrop potatoes, diced and cooked	175g
6oz	prawns	175g
¼pt	double cream	150ml
1 tblspn	whisky	1 × 15ml spn
	salt and black pepper	
2oz	Cheddar cheese, grated	50g

Method

1 **Fry** the onion gently in the butter until soft but not coloured.

2 **Add** the potatoes and prawns and continue cooking until everything is heated through.

3 **Pour** in the cream and whisky, season, then shake pan gently until the potatoes

and prawns are coated with the creamy whisky sauce.

4 **Spoon** into 4 small ramekin dishes and top with grated cheese.

5 **Flash** under a hot grill until the cheese is golden and bubbly.

6 **Serve** immediately.

North Sea Scallops

Ingredients
Serves 4

1¼lb	British potatoes, cooked and sieved	575g
2oz	butter	50g
2 tblspn	milk	2 × 15ml spn
8oz	haddock	225g
4oz	mushrooms, sliced	125g
1oz	plain flour	25g
½pt	milk	300ml
	salt and black pepper	
6oz	mature Cheddar cheese, grated	175g

Method

1 **Mix** the sieved potatoes with 1oz (25g) butter and the 2 tblspn (2 × 15ml spn) milk. Place in a piping bag fitted with a vegetable star nozzle and pipe a potato border round 4 shell dishes.

2 **Poach** the haddock in the milk for 10 minutes. Drain, reserving milk. Bone and flake the fish.

3 **In** a saucepan fry the mushrooms in the remaining

1oz (25g) butter, stir in the flour and cook for 1 minute. Gradually add the reserved milk and bring to the boil stirring continuously. Season.

4 **Add** the cheese and haddock to the sauce, heat through and pour into the centre of the shell dishes.

5 **Flash** under a hot grill until brown and bubbling. Serve.

Ham Salad Rolls

Ingredients
Serves 4

1lb	British potatoes, cooked and sieved	450g
2	spring onions, finely chopped	2
4	gherkins, chopped	4
1	egg, size 3, hard boiled and chopped	1
1 tspn	mild mustard	1 × 5ml spn
4 tblspn	mayonnaise	4 × 15ml spn
8oz can	apricots	220g can
	salt and black pepper	
8 slices	cooked ham	8 slices
	lettuce leaves	

Method

1 **Blend** together the potatoes, spring onions, gherkins, egg, mustard, mayonnaise and apricots reserving a few to garnish. Season to taste.

2 **Divide** the potato mixture between the 8 slices of cooked ham, spread the mixture to

within ½" (1cm) of the edge of each slice and roll up like a Swiss roll. Secure with cocktail sticks if necessary.

3 **Serve** on a bed of lettuce decorated with the remaining apricots.

Daylight falls from a circular roof lantern on to the solid beech kitchen table at Castle Drogo, in Devon.

Pictured from left:
Highland Prawns, Ham Salad Rolls, Smoked Mackerel Paté,
North Sea Scallops.

Meals for all the Family

For as long as anyone can remember the potato has been a part of the family meal. Unlike other vegetables, whose use may depend on personal likes and dislikes or on seasonal availability, the potato is seen as an essential ingredient in a well planned menu without which the meal would certainly not be complete. However, to provide a variation to the meal — that something a little different — in this chapter potato has been directly incorporated into the main dish by using potato pastry in some recipes. Of course, potato pastry is not a new idea — during the Second World War it was used widely to eke out and vary the meagre quantities of other ingredients available at that time — but if you have not tried it before I am sure you will agree that our recipe makes an excellent pastry. Naturally we have included potatoes in hotpots and casseroles which of course helps the meat to go a little further and don't forget to develop your skill with a piping bag by piping a border of potato round your favourite recipe to make it look even more appetising and attractive.

In the nursery at Wallington, near Morpeth, Northumberland.

A table ready to welcome guests to the restaurant at Saltram, Plymouth.

This open-fire range can be seen at The Georgian House, Edinburgh, and was used for roasting, grilling and much everyday cooking.

The piping of potato has been varied to show different designs.

Pictured from left:
Chicken and Broccoli Layer, Cider Fish Pie, Lamb Cobbler,
Beef and Ale Hotpot, Veal and Ham Pie.

Pictured from left:
Potato Fish Delight, Lamb Cobbler, Cider Fish Pie.

Potato Fish Delight

Ingredients		Serves 4
12oz	smoked haddock	350g
½pt	milk	300ml
1oz	butter	25g
1oz	plain flour	25g
4oz	mature Cheddar cheese, grated	125g
8oz	broccoli, cooked	225g
3	tomatoes, skinned and sliced	3
1lb	British potatoes, sliced and cooked	450g

Garnish: parsley

Cooking Temperature: 400°F, 200°C, Gas Mark 6

Method

1 **Poach** the fish in the milk until cooked. Strain, reserving the milk. Remove skin and flake the fish.

2 **Melt** the butter in a saucepan, stir in the flour and slowly add the reserved milk. Simmer for one minute. Stir in 2oz (50g) of the cheese and the fish.

3 **Place** the broccoli in a deep casserole dish, followed by the fish mixture. Layer the tomatoes on top and finish with a layer of potatoes.

4 **Sprinkle** with the remaining cheese. Bake in the oven for 30 minutes until golden brown.

5 **Serve** garnished with parsley.

Cider Fish Pie

Ingredients		Serves 4
1lb	smoked haddock	450g
½pt	milk	300ml
1	onion, finely chopped	1
2oz	butter or margarine	50g
4oz	mushrooms, sliced	125g
2oz	plain flour	50g
½pt	dry cider	300ml
	salt and black pepper	
3	eggs, size 3, hard boiled and sliced	3
2oz	butter, melted	25g
2 tblspn	milk	2 × 15ml spn
1½lb	British potatoes, cooked and sieved	675g

Cooking Temperature: 400°F, 200°C, Gas Mark 6

Method

1 **Poach** the haddock in the milk. Remove and flake the fish but do not discard the milk.

2 **Fry** the onion in the butter until soft, add the mushrooms and continue cooking for a further 2 minutes.

3 **Stir** in the flour and cook for 1 minute. Gradually add the reserved milk and the cider and bring to the boil stirring continuously.

4 **Fold** in the fish and season to taste.

5 **Put** half the mixture into a casserole dish, arrange the sliced eggs on top, then cover with the remainder of the fish mixture.

6 **Beat** the melted butter and the milk into the potatoes. Place in a piping bag fitted with a vegetable star nozzle and pipe the potato over the mixture.

7 **Bake,** uncovered, for 30 minutes until the potato is golden brown.

Lamb Cobbler

Ingredients		Serves 4
1 tblspn	oil	1 × 15ml spn
1lb	lamb fillet, cubed	450g
8oz	British potatoes, diced and parboiled	225g
6oz	button onions	175g
8oz can	chopped tomatoes	225g can
½ tspn	rosemary	1 × 2.5ml spn
¼pt	lamb stock	150ml
	salt and black pepper	
2 tblspn	cornflour	2 × 15ml spn
2 tblspn	water	2 × 15ml spn
Scone Topping		
8oz	plain flour	225g
pinch	salt	pinch
2 tspn	baking powder	2 × 5ml spn
1 tspn	mixed herbs	1 × 5ml spn
2oz	British potatoes, cooked and sieved	50g
2oz	margarine	50g
4fl oz	milk	120ml
1	egg, size 3, beaten to glaze	1

Garnish: parsley

Cooking Temperature: 350°F, 180°C, Gas Mark 4

Method

1 **Heat** the oil in a pan and fry the lamb until brown.

2 **Place** the lamb in a casserole dish with the potatoes, button onions, chopped tomatoes, rosemary, stock, salt and pepper.

3 **Cover** and cook at 350°F, 180°C, Gas Mark 4 for 45 minutes.

4 **Blend** the cornflour with the water until smooth, stir into the casserole. Return to the oven and continue cooking for a further 15 minutes.

5 **To make** the scone topping, sieve all the dry ingredients together and rub in the potatoes and margarine. Stir in the milk to form a soft dough.

6 **Roll** out the scone dough on a floured board until ½" (1cm) thick. Using a 2½" (6½cm) round cutter, cut out 8 scones.

7 **Place** on top of the lamb and brush with egg to glaze.

8 **Raise** the temperature to 400°F, 200°C, Gas Mark 6 and bake uncovered for 20 minutes..

9 **Serve** garnished with parsley.

The hearth occupies the whole width of the Great Kitchen at Compton Castle, near Torquay.

Beef and Ale Hotpot

Ingredients		Serves 4
1lb	braising steak, cubed	450g
2oz	plain flour	50g
1 tblspn	oil	1 × 15ml spn
1 large	onion, chopped	1 large
¼pt	ale	150ml
4oz	carrots, diced	125g
4oz	swede, diced	125g
4oz	button mushrooms	125g
	salt and black pepper	
1½lb	British potatoes, sliced and parboiled	675g
1	egg, size 3, beaten	1
	paprika	

Garnish: parsley, chopped

Cooking Temperature: 400°F, 200°C, Gas Mark 6

Method

1. **Toss** the meat in 1oz (25g) flour. Heat the oil in a pan and fry the meat until sealed. Remove and lay aside.
2. **Place** the onion in a pan and fry until soft. Stir in the remaining flour, then pour in the ale, stirring continuously. Add the carrots, swede, mushrooms and seasoning and return meat to the pan.
3. **Cover** and cook for 45 minutes until meat and vegetables are tender.
4. **Pour** into a deep casserole dish and layer the sliced potatoes on top in an overlapping pattern.
5. **Brush** with the beaten egg and sprinkle with a little paprika.
6. **Bake** uncovered, for 30 minutes until potatoes are golden brown.
7. **Serve** garnished with chopped parsley.

Rabbit Pie

Ingredients		Serves 4
8oz	rabbit meat, cubed	225g
1 small	onion, chopped	1 small
1oz	butter	25g
1oz	plain flour	25g
½pt	red wine	300ml
4oz	cooked ham, cubed	125g
4oz	carrots, sliced	125g
6oz	British potatoes, diced	175g
	salt and black pepper	
Pastry		
3oz	British potatoes, cooked and sieved	75g
6oz	plain flour	175g
1½oz	margarine	40g
1½oz	lard	40g
pinch	salt	pinch
1	egg, size 3, beaten, to glaze	1

Cooking Temperature: 400°F, 200°C, Gas Mark 6

Method

1. **Fry** the rabbit and onion in the butter. Stir in the flour, then the wine.
2. **Add** the ham, carrots, potatoes and seasoning. Simmer gently for 30 minutes and allow to cool.
3. **To** make the pastry, place all the ingredients in a bowl. Mix with a fork. Do not add water. Alternatively, a food processor can be used.
4. **Line** a 1pt (600ml) pie dish with two-thirds of the pastry and pour in filling. Top with remaining pastry.
5. **Brush** with egg and bake at 400°F, 200°C, Gas Mark 6 for 30 minutes. Reduce the temperature to 350°F, 180°C, Gas Mark 4 and continue baking for a further 30 minutes.

Veal and Ham Pie

Ingredients		Serves 4
Filling		
1	onion, finely chopped	1
4oz	button mushrooms	125g
2½oz	butter	65g
1½oz	plain flour	40g
¾pt	milk	450ml
8oz	British potatoes, diced and cooked	225g
1lb	veal, cooked and diced	450g
8oz	cooked ham, diced	225g
2	eggs, size 3, hard boiled and chopped	2
	salt and black pepper	
Pastry		
3oz	British potatoes, cooked and sieved	75g
6oz	plain flour	175g
1½oz	margarine	40g
1½oz	lard	40g
1½oz	Cheddar cheese, grated	40g
pinch	dry mustard	pinch
pinch	salt	pinch
1	egg, size 3, beaten, to glaze	1

Cooking Temperature: 400°F, 200°C, Gas Mark 6

Method

1. **Fry** the onion and mushrooms in the butter until soft.
2. **Stir** in the flour, then the milk. Bring to the boil, stirring continuously.
3. **Fold** in the potatoes, onion, mushrooms, veal, ham and eggs. Season to taste and pour into a 2pt (1.2ltr) pie dish or individual pie dishes.
4. **To** make the pastry, place all the ingredients in a bowl. Mix with a fork. Do not add water. Alternatively, a food processor can be used.
5. **Roll** out the pastry and cover the pie. Brush with beaten egg and bake for 40 minutes until golden brown.

Pictured from left:
Rabbit Pie, Beef and Ale Hotpot, Veal and Ham Pie.

Flying Saucers

Ingredients		Makes 4
Pastry		
6oz	British potatoes, cooked and sieved	175g
12oz	plain flour	350g
3oz	margarine	75g
3oz	lard	75g
pinch	salt	pinch
Filling		
12oz	minced beef	350g
1	onion, finely chopped	1
1	carrot, finely chopped	1
6oz	British potatoes, finely chopped	175g
4oz	mushrooms, sliced	125g
3 tblspn	tomato purée	3 × 15ml spn
¼pt	beef stock	150ml
	salt and black pepper	
	milk to glaze	

Garnish: 1 red pepper

Cooking Temperature: 400°F, 200°C, Gas Mark 6

Method

1 **To** make the pastry, place all the ingredients in a bowl. Mix with a fork. Do not add water. Alternatively, a food processor can be used.

2 **Roll** out the pastry and cut out eight circles. Use four of these to line four oven-proof saucers.

3 **Place** the minced beef in a pan and cook gently until browned. Add the onion and carrot and cook for a further 10-15 minutes.

4 **Add** the potatoes, mushrooms, tomato purée and stock. Season to taste, cover and simmer for 30 minutes, stirring occasionally.

5 **Using** a draining spoon, fill each saucer with the meat mixture. Brush the edges of the pastry with a little milk and place the pastry lid on top. Seal the pastry edges with a fork.

6 **Glaze** with milk and cook for 30 minutes.

7 **For** the garnish make the stars, by de-seeding the pepper and pressing it flat. Using small cutters, cut out the shapes. Place on the pies once cooked.

Kids Bubble & Squeak

Ingredients		Serves 4
2oz	butter	50g
1 small	onion, chopped	1 small
1lb	British potatoes, cooked and sieved	450g
6oz	peas, cooked	175g
6oz	sweetcorn, cooked	175g
	salt and black pepper	

Method

1 **Melt** the butter in a frying pan and fry onion until soft.

2 **Mix** the onion with the potatoes, peas and sweetcorn and season.

3 **Fry** the mixture until golden brown and crispy.

Jumbo Fish Cakes

Ingredients		Serves 4
1lb	British potatoes, cooked and sieved	450g
12oz	cod, cooked and flaked	350g
2 tblspn	parsley, chopped	2 × 15ml spn
4 tblspn	tomato ketchup	4 × 15ml spn
1 tblspn	lemon juice	1 × 15ml spn
	salt and black pepper	
1	egg, size 3, beaten to bind	1
1	egg, size 3, beaten to coat	1
6oz	crisps, crushed	175g
	oil for frying	

Method

1 **Mix** the potatoes, cod, parsley, tomato ketchup, lemon juice and seasoning together. Bind with one egg.

2 **Shape** into 4 cakes and coat with the remaining egg, followed by the crisps.

3 **Heat** the oil in a frying pan and fry the fish cakes until brown and crisp.

Double Deckers

Ingredients		Serves 4
1lb	British potatoes, cooked and sieved	450g
6oz	fresh breadcrumbs	175g
2 tspn	Worcestershire sauce	2 × 5ml spn
	salt and black pepper	
1	egg, size 3, beaten to coat	1
	oil for frying	
4	rashers back bacon	4
4	eggs	4

Method

1 **Mix** the potatoes, 2oz (50g) breadcrumbs, Worcestershire sauce and seasoning together.

2 **Roll** out onto a floured surface until ¼" (5mm) thick. Cut into eight rounds using a 3" (7.5cm) pastry cutter.

3 **Coat** the potato rounds in beaten egg and then cover with the remaining breadcrumbs.

4 **Fry** the potato rounds in a little oil until they are crisp and light golden brown.

5 **Meanwhile** grill the bacon and fry the eggs.

6 **Sandwich** one egg and one rasher of bacon between two of the potato rounds. Repeat a further three times and serve immediately.

Pictured from left:
Kids Bubble and Squeak, Flying Saucers, Jumbo Fish Cakes,
Double Deckers.

Pictured from left:
Chicken and Broccoli Layer, Pork and Orange Casserole,
Spicy Lamb Pie.

Pork and Orange Casserole

Ingredients
Serves 4

1lb	pork fillet, sliced	450g
2 tblspn	plain flour	2 × 15ml spn
	salt and black pepper	
1 tblspn	oil	1 × 15ml spn
1oz	butter	25g
1	onion, chopped	1
1	red pepper, chopped	1
12oz	British potatoes, diced	350g
1 tblspn	tomato purée	1 × 15ml spn
1	orange, rind and juice	1
½pt	cider	300ml
2 tspn	Herbs de Provence	2 × 5ml spn
7¾oz can	pineapple chunks and juice	220g can

Garnish: parsley, chopped

Cooking Temperature: 375°F, 190°C, Gas Mark 5

Method

1 **Place** the pork fillet, 1 tblspn (1 × 15ml spn) flour, salt and black pepper in a plastic bag and shake.

2 **Heat** the oil and butter together in a large frying pan, add the contents of the plastic bag and fry until browned.

3 **Remove** from the pan and transfer to a casserole dish.

4 **Fry** the onion and pepper gently until just softened. Add the potatoes and fry for a further 5 minutes.

5 **Stir** in the remaining flour, tomato purée, orange rind and juice, cider, herbs and pineapple juice. Bring to the boil and pour over the pork fillets.

6 **Bake** in the oven for 1 hour, add the pineapple chunks to the casserole and then cook for a further 30 minutes.

7 **Serve** hot sprinkled with chopped parsley.

Chicken and Broccoli Layer

Ingredients
Serves 4

10.4oz can	condensed chicken soup	295g can
6 tblspn	mayonnaise	6 × 15ml spn
7fl oz	milk	210ml
	salt and black pepper	
1lb	fresh broccoli, cooked and finely chopped	450g
12oz	chicken, cooked and diced	350g
1lb	British potatoes, sliced and parboiled	450g
6oz	Red Leicester cheese, grated	175g

Garnish: parsley, chopped

Cooking Temperature: 400°F, 200°C, Gas Mark 6

Method

1 **Mix** the soup, mayonnaise, milk and seasoning together.

2 **Pour** half of the soup mixture into a shallow casserole dish. Arrange broccoli evenly over the soup, then the chicken and finally the sliced potatoes.

3 **Pour** remaining sauce over the potatoes and cook for 30 minutes.

4 **Sprinkle** the cheese on top and cook for a further 15 minutes.

5 **Serve** garnished with chopped parsley.

Spicy Lamb Pie

Ingredients
Serves 4-6

Filling

1 tblspn	oil	1 × 15ml spn
1	onion, chopped	1
1 clove	garlic, crushed	1 clove
1lb	minced lamb	450g
2 tblspn	plain flour	2 × 15ml spn
1 tblspn	tomato purée	1 × 15ml spn
14oz can	tomatoes	400g can
¼pt	lamb stock	150ml
	salt and black pepper	
1	orange, grated rind	1
2 tblspn	orange juice	2 × 15ml spn
pinch	nutmeg	pinch
½ tspn	cumin	1 × 2.5ml spn
½ tspn	ground coriander	1 × 2.5ml spn
1	egg, size 3, beaten, to glaze	1
12oz	British potatoes, sliced and parboiled	350g

Potato Pastry

4oz	British potatoes, cooked and sieved	125g
4oz	plain flour	125g
4oz	wholemeal flour	125g
2oz	margarine	50g
2oz	lard	50g
pinch	salt	pinch

Cooking Temperature: 400°F, 200°C, Gas Mark 6

Method

1 **Heat** the oil in a large pan, add the onion, garlic and mince and fry until the meat is brown and the onion is soft.

2 **Stir** in the flour, tomato purée, tomatoes, stock and seasoning and bring to the boil.

3 **Add** the orange rind and juice, spices and herbs. Simmer for 15 minutes. Allow to cool.

4 **To** make the pastry, place all the ingredients in a bowl. Mix with a fork. Do not add water. Alternatively, a food processor can be used.

5 **Use** two-thirds of the pastry to line a 9″ (23cm) pie dish. Roll out the remaining pastry to form a lid.

6 **Brush** the edges of the pastry with the beaten egg, spoon half the lamb mixture into the case and place the potato slices on top. Spoon remaining lamb mixture over the potato slices.

7 **Put** the lid in place, seal and brush with beaten egg.

8 **Bake** for 30 minutes until golden brown.

Tasty Turnovers

Ingredients		Makes 6
Filling		
1	onion, finely chopped	1
1 tblspn	oil	1 × 15ml spn
12oz	pork mince	350g
6oz	British potatoes, finely diced	175g
1 tblspn	plain flour	1 × 15ml spn
2 tspn	Herbs de Provence	2 × 5ml spn
1	orange, rind and juice	1
	salt and black pepper	
½pt	chicken stock	300ml
2oz	sultanas	50g
Pastry		
6oz	British potatoes, cooked and sieved	175g
12oz	plain flour	350g
3oz	margarine	75g
3oz	lard	75g
pinch	salt	pinch
1	egg, size 3, beaten to glaze	1
Cooking Temperature: 400°F, 200°C, Gas Mark 6		

Method

1 **Fry** the onion in the oil until softened, add the pork and fry until browned. Finally add the potatoes and fry for 5 minutes.

2 **Stir** in the flour and cook for 1-2 minutes, then add all the remaining ingredients and simmer for 15 minutes until the mixture has thickened. Leave to cool.

3 **To** make the pastry, place all the ingredients in a bowl. Mix with a fork. Do not add water. Alternatively, a food processor can be used.

4 **Divide** the pastry into 6 and shape into 7″ (18cm) rounds.

5 **Place** one sixth of the filling onto a round of pastry, brush around the edge with beaten egg. Fold one half of the pastry over and seal to make the turnover. Repeat five times and place onto a greased baking tray.

6 **Brush** with beaten egg and place in the oven for 30 minutes or until browned. Serve hot or cold with a salad.

Chunky Beef Hotpot

Ingredients		Serves 4
2oz	plain flour	50g
	salt and black pepper	
1lb	stewing beef, cubed	450g
2 tblspn	oil	2 × 15ml spn
2	onions, sliced	2
12oz	carrots, sliced	350g
½ tspn	dried thyme	1 × 2.5ml spn
1pt	beef stock	600ml
1½lb	British potatoes, sliced	675g
1oz	butter, melted	25g
Cooking Temperature: 325°F, 170°C, Gas Mark 3		

Method

1 **Toss** the meat in seasoned flour.

2 **Heat** the oil and fry the meat briskly until well browned. Remove to a casserole.

3 **Reduce** the heat and fry the onions and carrots gently for 5 minutes. Transfer to the casserole.

4 **Sprinkle** the thyme and seasoning over the meat and vegetables then pour in the stock.

5 **Overlap** the potatoes in a neat layer on top.

6 **Brush** with melted butter and bake uncovered at 325°F, 170°C, Gas Mark 3 for 2 hours. Increase the heat to 400°F, 200°C, Gas Mark 6 and cook for a further 30 minutes until the potatoes are golden brown.

Pork Chops with Pineapple Sauce

Ingredients		Serves 4
4	pork chops	4
3oz	butter	75g
7¾oz can	pineapple slices in natural juice	220g can
1	egg, size 3, beaten	1
1½lb	British potatoes, cooked and sieved	675g
1oz	plain flour	25g
½ tspn	dry mustard	1 × 2.5ml spn
¼pt	cider	150ml
	salt and black pepper	
Garnish: glacé cherries, parsley		
Cooking Temperature: 375°F, 190°C, Gas Mark 5		

Method

1 **Place** the pork chops in a roasting tin and dot with 1oz (25g) of butter, season.

2 **Bake** uncovered for 45 minutes, turning once during cooking.

3 **Drain** the pineapple slices, reserving juice. Remove roasting tin from oven and place a pineapple slice on each chop. Return to the oven for a further 15 minutes.

4 **Meanwhile** beat the remaining 2oz (50g) butter and all but 2 tspn (2 × 5ml spn) of the beaten egg into the potato. Season to taste.

5 **Place** mixture into a piping bag fitted with a vegetable star nozzle and pipe a border round an ovenproof serving dish.

6 **Brush** potato border with remaining beaten egg and place under a hot grill until browned.

7 **Remove** the chops from the oven and arrange in the centre of the serving dish.

8 **Stir** the flour and mustard into the fat left in the roasting tin and gradually add the cider.

9 **Pour** the sauce over the chops and serve garnished with glacé cherries and parsley.

35

Pictured from left:
Tasty Turnovers, Chunky Beef Hotpot,
Pork Chops with Pineapple Sauce.

Pictured from left:
Kidneys in Ale Sauce, Sausage Hotpot, Cider Chicken Pie.

Cider Chicken Pie

Ingredients
Serves 4

Filling

1oz	butter	25g
1 tblspn	oil	1 × 15ml spn
12oz	British potatoes, diced	350g
1lb	chicken, cooked and diced	450g
1 large	onion, chopped	1 large
2 sticks	celery, chopped	2 sticks
4oz	mushrooms, sliced	125g
2oz	plain flour	50g
½pt	cider	300ml
½pt	chicken stock	300ml
1 tspn	mixed herbs	1 × 5ml spn
	salt and pepper	
1 tblspn	fresh parsley, chopped	1 × 15ml spn

Pastry

3oz	British potatoes, cooked and sieved	75g
6oz	plain flour	175g
1½oz	margarine	40g
1½oz	lard	40g
pinch	salt	pinch
1	egg, size 3, beaten, to glaze	1

Cooking Temperature: 400°F, 200°C, Gas Mark 6

Method

1 To make the filling, heat the butter and oil in a large pan and add the potatoes, chicken, onion, celery and mushrooms. Fry until the vegetables are beginning to soften.

2 **Stir** in the flour, then gradually add the cider and stock, stirring continuously. Add the remaining ingredients and simmer for 15 minutes, stirring occasionally. Pour into a large ovenproof dish or individual pie dishes and leave to cool.

3 To make the pastry place all the ingredients in a bowl. Mix with a fork. Do not add water. Alternatively, a food processor can be used.

4 **Roll** out the pastry to make a lid for the chicken filling. Glaze with egg. Use the trimmings to garnish the pie.

5 **Bake** for about 30 minutes until the pastry is golden brown. Serve hot.

Sausage Hotpot

Ingredients
Serves 4

1 large	onion, finely chopped	1 large
1	green pepper, diced	1
2oz	butter	50g
10.4oz can	condensed vegetable soup	295g can
1lb	spicy sausages, grilled	450g
1½lb	British potatoes, sliced and parboiled	675g
	grill seasoning	

Cooking Temperature: 400°F, 200°C, Gas Mark 6

Method

1 **Fry** the onion and pepper in 1oz (25g) of butter until soft but not brown.

2 **Mix** the soup with half the recommended water, add the sausages, onion and green pepper, mix well and place in a casserole dish.

3 **Arrange** the sliced potatoes on top. Melt remaining 1oz (25g) of butter and brush the sliced potatoes.

4 **Sprinkle** with grill seasoning and cook in oven for 30-40 minutes until potatoes are golden brown.

Kidneys in Ale Sauce

Ingredients
Serves 4

10	lambs kidneys	10
1oz	butter	25g
1	onion, chopped	1
4oz	bacon, chopped	125g
1oz	plain flour	25g
2 tspn	French mustard	2 × 5ml spn
1 tblspn	tomato purée	1 × 15ml spn
1 tspn	demerara sugar	1 × 5ml spn
9fl oz	ale	275ml
	salt and black pepper	
1½lb	British potatoes, cooked and sieved	675g
1½oz	butter	40g
1 tspn	mixed herbs	1 × 5ml spn
¼pt	single cream	150ml

Garnish: parsley, chopped

Method

1 **Sauté** the kidneys in the butter for 2-3 minutes. Add the onion and bacon and continue to cook gently until the onion is transparent.

2 **Stir** in the flour and cook for a further minute. Add the mustard, tomato purée and sugar, mix thoroughly.

3 **Gradually** pour in the ale, stirring continuously. Season to taste.

4 **Bring** to the boil and simmer for 15 minutes.

5 **Mix** together the sieved potatoes, butter and mixed herbs. Place in a piping bag fitted with a vegetable star nozzle and pipe a border round the serving dish. Flash under a hot grill until browned.

6 **Stir** the cream into the kidney mixture and heat gently.

7 **Pour** into the centre of the serving dish and garnish with parsley.

The kitchen of the famous eighteenth century dolls' house at Uppark, West Sussex.

Supper Dishes

The days of the log fire or even the coal fire are now largely gone and although some may regret the passing of the evenings when one could sit around the glowing embers, few who had the chore of cleaning the dusty remains the following morning will mourn the passing of this form of heating, which was often more successful in raising the temperature of the chimney than of the room. Nowadays most of us have some form of central heating installed which whilst being ideal for the outsides of our bodies does little for the 'inner man'. This of course is where potatoes really score for what for instance could be easier, or more nutritious, than jacket baked potatoes containing your favourite fillings. Potatoes are the original convenience food so baking your potatoes maximises this natural packaging, with which every potato comes, in the simplest and most economical way. Don't forget, with most of the vitamins and dietary fibre located just under the skin it's an absolute sin to throw the skin away. From the following pages choose fillings from chilli, sausages, beans — use the one you like best — *with baked potatoes the choice really is yours'!* The preparation and cooking times for jacket potatoes are given in this chapter on Page 41.

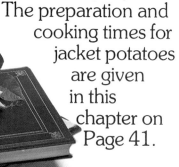

At Lanhydrock, near Bodmin, this is the room where Lady Robartes would conduct household business.

Plates line a kitchen dresser at Saltram, Plymouth.

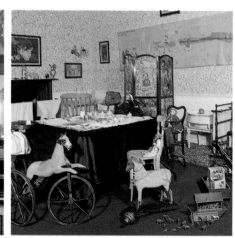

Teatime in the nursery at Wallington, near Morpeth, Northumberland.

Pictured from left:
Ham and Mushroom Pancakes, Potato Medley, Chicken and Potato au Gratin, Chilli Bakes, Prawn Bakes.

Pictured from left:
Chicken and Mushroom Pie, Potato Medley, Prawn Bakes.

Prawn Bakes

Ingredients — Serves 4

4 × 8oz	British potatoes, scrubbed and baked	4 × 225g
1oz	butter	25g
1oz	plain flour	25g
¼pt	milk	150ml
2fl oz	white wine	60ml
6oz	prawns	175g
	salt and black pepper	

Method

1 **Melt** the butter in a saucepan and stir in the flour.
2 **Gradually** add the milk and bring slowly to the boil, stirring continuously.
3 **Stir** in the wine and prawns and season to taste.
4 **Make** a crosswise incision in the potatoes and open out by pressing at the base of the potatoes.
5 **Divide** the filling between the potatoes.

Chicken and Mushroom Pie

Ingredients — Serves 4

6oz	mushrooms, sliced	175g
2	leeks, sliced	2
2½oz	butter	65g
2oz	flour	50g
¾pt	milk	450ml
8oz	British potatoes, diced and cooked	225g
8oz	chicken, cooked and diced	225g
	salt and black pepper	

Pastry

4oz	British potatoes, cooked and sieved	125g
8oz	plain flour	225g
2oz	margarine	50g
2oz	lard	50g
pinch	salt	pinch
1	egg, size 3, beaten	1

Cooking Temperature: 400°F, 200°C, Gas Mark 6

Method

1 **Fry** the mushrooms and leeks in the butter for 5 minutes.
2 **Add** the flour and gradually add the milk, stirring continuously. Bring to the boil.
3 **Stir** in the potatoes and chicken and season to taste. Allow to cool.
4 **Whilst** the filling is cooling, make the pastry by placing all the ingredients in a bowl. Mix with a fork. Do not add water.

Alternatively, a food processor can be used.
5 **Roll** out two-thirds of the pastry and line a 2pt (1.2 ltr) pie dish or four individual pie dishes.
6 **Place** filling in dish/dishes and roll out remaining pastry to cover the pie/pies. Brush with beaten egg and cook for 30 minutes or until golden brown in colour.

Baked Potatoes

Wash the potatoes thoroughly and bake in a pre-heated oven at 425°F, 220°C, Gas Mark 7 for 1-1½ hours. A baked potato spike or skewer can be used and will cut the cooking time down by about 15 minutes.

Potato Medley

Ingredients — Serves 4-6

6oz	bacon, chopped	175g
2lb	British potatoes, sliced	900g
	salt and black pepper	
2oz	butter	50g
1 large	onion, thinly sliced	1 large
8oz	Gouda cheese, grated	225g
¼pt	single cream	150ml

Garnish: parsley

Cooking Temperature: 350°F, 180°C, Gas Mark 5

Method

1 **Fry** the bacon.
2 **Layer** one-third of the potatoes in the bottom of a large casserole dish. Season with salt and black pepper and dot with ½oz (15g) butter.
3 **Place** one-third of the onion, bacon and cheese over the potatoes and dot with butter.
4 **Repeat** methods 2 and 3 twice more and finally pour over the cream and season again.
5 **Cover** and cook for one hour. Remove the lid and cook for a further half an hour to brown the cheese.
6 **Serve** hot garnished with parsley.

These spectacular Chinese porcelain tureens, modelled as geese, can be seen at Brodick Castle, Isle of Arran.

Pictured from left:
Crunchy Carrot Bakes, Sausage and Bean Bakes, Chilli Bakes.

Crunchy Carrot Bakes

Ingredients		Serves 4
4 × 8oz	British potatoes, scrubbed and baked	4 × 225g
1	green apple	1
1 tblspn	lemon juice	1 × 15ml spn
6oz	carrots, grated	175g
4oz	cheese, grated	125g
2oz	hazelnuts, chopped	50g
2oz	sultanas	50g
	salt and black pepper	

Garnish: parsley

Method

1 **Dice** the apple and sprinkle with lemon juice.
2 **Place** the carrot and cheese in a bowl. Add the apple, hazelnuts and sultanas, season and mix well.
3 **Make** a crosswise incision in the potatoes and open out by pressing at the base of the potatoes.
4 **Divide** the filling between the potatoes and serve garnished with parsley.

Sausage and Bean Bakes

Ingredients		Serves 4
4 × 8oz	British potatoes, scrubbed and baked	4 × 225g
8oz	sausages	225g
15.9oz can	baked beans	450g can
1 tspn	mixed herbs	1 × 5ml spn
	salt and black pepper	

Garnish: parsley

Method

1 **Grill** the sausages, then cut into quarters.
2 **Place** the baked beans in a saucepan with the sausages, mixed herbs and seasoning. Simmer for 5 minutes, stirring occasionally.
3 **Make** a crosswise incision in the potatoes and open out by pressing at the base of the potatoes.
4 **Divide** the filling between the potatoes and serve garnished with parsley.

Chilli Bakes

Ingredients		Serves 4
4 × 8oz	British potatoes, scrubbed and baked	4 × 225g
12oz	minced beef	350g
1	onion, chopped	1
1oz	butter	25g
2oz	mushrooms, sliced	50g
2 tblspn	tomato purée	2 × 15ml spn
1	beef stock cube	1
1 tblspn	water	1 × 15ml spn
1-2 tspn	chilli powder	1-2 × 5ml spn
8¾oz can	red kidney beans, drained and rinsed	248g can
	salt and black pepper	

Garnish: parsley

Method

1 **Fry** the minced beef and drain off fat, place beef in a saucepan.
2 **Fry** the onion in the butter until soft but not brown, add to saucepan with mushrooms, tomato purée, stock cube and water. Cover and simmer for 20 minutes.
3 **Add** chilli powder, red kidney beans and seasoning, stir well and simmer, covered, for a further 10 minutes.
4 **Make** a crosswise incision in the potatoes and open out by pressing at the base of the potatoes.
5 **Divide** the filling between the potatoes and serve garnished with parsley.

The Hall at Cotehele House, Cornwall, depicted by the nineteenth century Plymouth artist, Condy.

Potato Pie

Ingredients		Serves 4
1½lb	British potatoes, cooked and mashed	675g
2oz	butter	50g
1	egg, size 3	1
large pinch	nutmeg	large pinch
	salt and pepper	
8oz	Cheddar cheese, grated	225g
2	tomatoes, sliced	2

Garnish: parsley, chopped

Cooking Temperature: 400°F, 200°C, Gas Mark 6

Method

1 **Beat** the potato, butter, egg, nutmeg and seasoning together. Beat in 6oz (175g) of the cheese.

2 **Place** in a casserole dish and arrange sliced tomatoes on top. Sprinkle with remaining cheese.

3 **Bake** for 20 minutes until golden brown. Serve hot, garnished with chopped parsley.

Leeks in Cheese Sauce

Ingredients		Serves 4
4	leeks, trimmed and cut into 1″ (2½cm) lengths	4
8oz	streaky bacon, chopped	225g
1lb	British potatoes, diced and cooked	450g
1oz	butter	25g
1oz	plain flour	25g
½pt	milk	300ml
3oz	Cheddar cheese, grated	75g
2	eggs, size 3, yolks	2
	salt and pepper	

Garnish: parsley

Cooking Temperature: 350°F, 180°C, Gas Mark 4

Method

1 **Cook** the leeks in boiling salted water for 10 minutes. Drain.

2 **Heat** a frying pan and fry the bacon. Add the potatoes and continue cooking for 5 minutes.

3 **Arrange** the leeks on the base of a shallow pie dish, then scatter the bacon and potatoes over them.

4 **Prepare** the cheese sauce by melting the butter in a small saucepan, stir in the flour then gradually add the milk, stirring continuously until the mixture comes to the boil.

5 **Remove** from the heat, stir in the cheese and egg yolks and season to taste.

6 **Pour** the sauce over the contents of the pie dish and bake uncovered for 35-40 minutes until well browned.

7 **Serve** hot garnished with parsley.

Ham and Mushroom Pancakes

Ingredients		Serves 4
Filling		
1½oz	butter	40g
4oz	mushrooms, sliced	125g
1½oz	plain flour	40g
¾pt	milk	450ml
8oz	British potatoes, diced and cooked	225g
12oz	cooked ham, chopped	350g
	salt and black pepper	
Batter		
4oz	plain flour	125g
pinch	salt	pinch
1	egg, size 3, beaten	1
½pt	milk	300ml
3 tblspn	oil for frying	3 × 15ml spn

Garnish: parsley, chopped

Method

1 **Melt** the butter in a saucepan and add the mushrooms. Fry until soft.

2 **Add** the flour and cook for 1 minute. Remove from heat and gradually add the milk. Return to heat and bring to the boil, stirring until thickened. Add the potatoes and ham, season to taste. Keep the sauce hot.

3 **To make** the batter, sieve together the flour and salt and place in a bowl. Make a well in the centre and mix in the egg.

4 **Gradually** add the milk, beating well. Allow to stand for 30 minutes.

5 **Lightly** oil an 8″ (20cm) frying pan. Heat and pour in enough of the batter to thinly cover the base. Allow to brown on the base and then flip the pancake over and cook the other side.

6 **Repeat** this method until all the batter has been used.

7 **Layer** the pancakes with greaseproof paper and keep warm on a plate over a pan of hot water.

8 **Once** all the pancakes have been made, place equal amounts of filling on the pancakes and roll them up. Serve hot, garnished with chopped parsley.

An inscription in the servants' passage at Erddig, near Wrexham, prays for the household's protection.

Pictured from left:
Ham and Mushroom Pancakes, Potato Pie, Leeks in Cheese
Sauce.

Pictured from left:
Tuna Crunch, Liver Stir Fry, Chicken and Potato au Gratin.

Liver Stir Fry

Ingredients   Serves 4

1oz	butter	25g
1	leek, chopped	1
1 clove	garlic, crushed	1 clove
1lb	lambs liver, sliced thinly and cut into strips	450g
8oz	British potatoes, grated and rinsed	225g
4oz	streaky bacon, chopped	125g
1	red pepper, chopped	1
2 tspn	soy sauce	2 × 5ml spn
1 tspn	Worcestershire sauce	1 × 5ml spn
2 tblspn	sherry	2 × 15ml spn
	salt and black pepper	

Method

1 **Melt** the butter in a large frying pan or wok and fry the leek, garlic and liver for 3 minutes.
2 **Add** the potatoes, bacon and pepper and fry for a further 5 minutes, stirring from time to time.
3 **Add** the soy sauce, Worcestershire sauce, sherry and seasoning and fry for a further 2 minutes.

Tuna Crunch

Ingredients   Serves 4

1 tblspn	oil	1 × 15ml spn
½	green pepper, diced	½
3oz	mushrooms, sliced	75g
1½oz	butter	40g
1½oz	plain flour	40g
¾pt	milk	450ml
½ tspn	English mustard	1 × 2.5ml spn
	salt and black pepper	
7oz can	tuna fish, drained	198g can
1½lb	British potatoes, cut into chunks and cooked	675g
4oz	cheese, grated	125g
Topping		
1oz	butter	25g
2oz	plain crisps, crushed	50g

Cooking Temperature: 375°F, 190°C, Gas Mark 5

Method

1 **Heat** the oil in a large saucepan. Add the pepper and mushrooms. Fry gently until soft. Remove from the pan.
2 **Melt** the butter in the same saucepan. Stir in the flour and cook over a low heat for 1 minute, gradually add the milk stirring continuously until the sauce comes to the boil and thickens.
3 **Add** the mustard, seasoning, tuna fish, pepper, mushrooms and potatoes. Remove from the heat and stir in the cheese. Transfer to an ovenproof dish.
4 **To make** the topping, melt the butter, then stir in the crisps until they are well coated. Spoon them over the tuna mixture to form an even layer.
5 **Bake** in the oven for about 20 minutes until the crisps are golden brown. Serve hot.

Chicken and Potato au Gratin

Ingredients   Serves 4

3 tblspn	oil	3 × 15ml spn
1	onion, chopped	1
2 cloves	garlic, crushed	2 cloves
12oz	chicken breasts, cut into strips	350g
1	green pepper, chopped	1
1	red pepper, chopped	1
2	courgettes, sliced	2
14oz can	tomatoes, chopped	400g can
1	bay leaf	1
1 tblspn	cornflour	1 × 15ml spn
1 tblspn	water	1 × 15ml spn
	salt and black pepper	
1lb	British potatoes, sliced and parboiled	450g
3oz	Red Leicester cheese, grated	75g

Cooking Temperature: 400°F, 200°C, Gas Mark 6

Method

1 **Heat** the oil in a large frying pan. Fry the onion and garlic until transparent. Add the chicken and seal the flesh.
2 **Add** the peppers and cook for a further 10 minutes. Stir in the courgettes, tomatoes and bay leaf.
3 **In** a small bowl blend the cornflour and water to make a smooth paste. Pour this into the pan and mix thoroughly.
4 **Season** and simmer for 35 minutes, stirring regularly. Remove bay leaf, transfer to a casserole dish and layer the potatoes on top. Season and cover with grated cheese.
5 **Bake** in a pre-heated oven for 30 minutes until the potatoes are cooked and the cheese is golden brown.

All Year Entertaining

The days of the British reticence, of a desire to keep to oneself are fast disappearing. An Englishman's home may still be his castle but nowadays he is much keener to share his castle — for a few hours anyway — with his friends and relatives. As a result entertaining at home has increased to such an extent that hosts would not let their friends leave without them tasting their culinary skills.

Of course entertaining takes different forms — from the casual snack to the multi-course dinner with the finger buffet and party nibbles falling somewhere in between but whatever your requirement this chapter should provide the answer. So that you may ring the changes on many of the recipes, the potatoes have been cooked in a variety of ways which will bring interest to you during preparation and delight your guests during the meal. A word of warning though! Tempting as it may be to prepare your potatoes well in advance, to allow plenty of time for that pre-dinner drink, remember that potatoes start to lose their nutrients if kept too long before cooking or serving.

The elegant dining room, with Victorian oak ceiling and fireplace, at Drum Castle, near Aberdeen.

Mid-eighteenth century Chelsea porcelain tureen shaped like a plaice, from a pair at Erddig, near Wrexham.

The kitchen of Castle Drogo, built on a Devonshire hilltop to designs by Sir Edwin Lutyens.

Pictured from left:
Duchesse Potatoes, Crown Roast of Lamb, Cheesy Caraway
Rolls, Cheese and Prawn Flans, Crispy Beef Stroganoff.

Neptune Soufflé

Ingredients

		Serves 4
8oz	cod fillet, skinned	225g
½pt	milk	300ml
½	onion, chopped	½
1 small	carrot, chopped	1 small
1	bay leaf	1
2oz	butter	50g
3oz	plain flour	75g
¼pt	single cream	150ml
4	eggs, size 3, separated	4
1lb	British potatoes, diced and cooked	450g
	salt and black pepper	
½ tspn	cayenne pepper	1 × 2.5ml spn
2oz	Cheddar cheese	50g

Cooking Temperature: 400°F, 200°C, Gas Mark 6

Method

1 **Poach** the fish in the milk for 10 minutes with the onion, carrot and bay leaf.

2 **Drain** and flake the fish, reserving the milk but discarding the vegetables.

3 **Make** the sauce by melting the butter and stirring in the flour. Cook for 2 minutes. Gradually add the reserved milk and the cream. Bring to the boil, stirring continuously.

4 **Beat** in the egg yolks then fold in the fish and potatoes. Season to taste and add the cayenne pepper.

5 **Whisk** the egg whites until stiff and fold into the sauce mixture. Pour into a greased 2pt (1.2 ltr) soufflé dish.

6 **Sprinkle** with the cheese and bake in the oven for 40-45 minutes until risen and golden brown. Serve.

Chicken in Creamy Apple Sauce

Ingredients

		Serves 4
Filling		
2 tblspn	oil	2 × 15ml spn
4	chicken breasts	4
1	onion, chopped	1
1 clove	garlic, crushed	1 clove
1oz	flour	25g
¼pt	apple sauce	150ml
¼pt	chicken stock	150ml
¼pt	cider	150ml
1 tspn	tarragon	1 × 5ml spn
	salt and black pepper	
¼pt	double cream	150ml
Border		
1½lb	British potatoes, cooked and sieved	675g
2oz	butter	50g
Garnish: parsley		

Cooking Temperature: 350°F, 180°C, Gas Mark 4

Method

1 **Heat** the oil and brown the chicken breasts on both sides. Remove to a casserole.

2 **Sauté** the onion and garlic in the remaining oil for 2-3 minutes.

3 **Stir** in the flour, then gradually add the apple sauce, stock, cider and tarragon, stirring continuously until the sauce reaches boiling point. Season to taste.

4 **Pour** the sauce over the chicken. Cover and cook in the oven for 1 hour.

5 **When** the chicken is almost ready, beat the butter into the potatoes. Place in a piping bag fitted with a vegetable star nozzle and pipe a double border of potato round a shallow serving dish. Flash under a hot grill.

6 **Remove** the chicken from the oven and arrange within the potato border. Stir the cream into the sauce and pour over the chicken.

7 **Garnish** with parsley.

Lamb Noisettes in Pastry

Ingredients

		Serves 4
4	lamb noisettes	4
1oz	butter	25g
pinch	lamb seasoning	pinch
sprinkle	dried mint	sprinkle
	salt and black pepper	
4oz	paté	125g
Pastry		
4oz	British potatoes, cooked and sieved	125g
8oz	plain flour	225g
2oz	margarine	50g
2oz	lard	50g
pinch	salt	pinch
1	egg, size 3, beaten to glaze	1

Cooking temperature: 400°F, 200°C, Gas Mark 6

Method

1 **Dot** the noisettes with butter and season with the lamb seasoning, dried mint, salt and pepper.

2 **Place** under a hot grill and cook for 10 minutes, turning once. Allow to cool.

3 **To** make the pastry, place all the ingredients in a bowl. Mix with a fork. Do not add water. Alternatively, a food processor can be used.

4 **Divide** the pastry into 4 and roll out each piece to measure 5″ x 5″ (13cm x 13cm).

5 **Place** a noisette in the centre of each pastry square and top with paté.

6 **Fold** over each pastry square to form 4 parcels and seal the edges well.

7 **Brush** with beaten egg and bake for 30-40 minutes until golden brown.

Tiny hallmarked silver vessels crowd the table of the dolls' house dining room at Uppark, West Sussex.

51

Pictured from left:
Lamb Noisettes in Pastry, Neptune Soufflé, Chicken in Creamy
Apple Sauce.

52

Pictured from left:
Turkey de Luxe, Crown Roast of Lamb, Veal Escalopes.

Veal Escalopes

Ingredients
		Serves 4
1½oz	plain flour	40g
½ tspn	paprika	1 × 2.5ml spn
	salt and black pepper	
12oz	British potatoes, sliced and parboiled	350g
4 × 4oz	veal escalopes, beaten	4 × 125g
1	egg, size 3, beaten	1
2oz	dried breadcrumbs	50g
2oz	butter	50g
2 tblspn	oil	2 × 15ml spn
4 slices	processed cheese	4 slices

Garnish: watercress

Method

1 **Place** ½oz (15g) flour in a small polythene bag with paprika and seasoning. Shake the sliced potatoes in the mixture.

2 **Coat** the veal escalopes in the remaining flour, then in egg and finally in breadcrumbs.

3 **Heat** the butter and oil in a frying pan and fry the veal escalopes until golden brown on both sides, approximately 5 minutes each side. Drain and keep warm.

4 **Place** the potato slices in the frying pan and fry until golden brown on both sides. Drain.

5 **Place** a layer of sliced potatoes on each veal escalope then top with a slice of cheese.

6 **Grill** until cheese just starts to melt. Serve garnished with watercress.

Turkey de Luxe

Ingredients
		Serves 4
4 × 6oz	turkey fillets	4 × 175g
3oz	butter	75g
2	onions, finely chopped	2
4oz	button mushrooms, sliced	125g
1½oz	plain flour	40g
½pt	milk	300ml
¼pt	white wine	150ml
1 tblspn	parsley, chopped	1 × 15ml spn
¼pt	double cream	150ml
Duchesse Mixture		
1½lb	British potatoes, cooked and sieved	675g
2oz	butter	50g
1	egg, size 3	1
pinch	nutmeg	pinch
	salt and black pepper	

Garnish: parsley, chopped

Method

1 **Season** the turkey fillets.

2 **Melt** the butter and fry the onions gently until soft. Add the mushrooms and fry for 1 minute. Add the turkey fillets and cook lightly on each side to seal. Remove from the frying pan.

3 **Stir** in the flour and cook gently. Gradually stir in the milk and bring to the boil, stirring continuously.

4 **Add** the wine and stir in the parsley. Replace the turkey fillets, cover and simmer gently for 30 minutes, turning the turkey fillets over twice until tender.

5 **While** the turkey fillets are cooking, beat the butter, egg, nutmeg and seasoning into the sieved potato. Place in a piping bag fitted with a vegetable star nozzle and pipe a potato border round the edge of an oval serving dish. Flash under a hot grill.

6 **Season** the sauce to taste and stir in the cream. Arrange the turkey fillets in the centre of the serving dish and cover with the sauce.

7 **Garnish** with chopped parsley.

Crown Roast of Lamb

Ingredients
		Serves 4-6
1	crown of lamb containing 12-14 cutlets this can be ordered from your local butcher	1
1oz	butter, melted	25g
	lamb seasoning	
Stuffing		
1	onion, finely chopped	1
2 sticks	celery, finely chopped	2 sticks
1oz	butter	25g
8oz	British potatoes, cooked and sieved	225g
2oz	dried apricots, finely chopped	50g
½ tspn	marjoram	1 × 2.5ml spn
½ tspn	rosemary	1 × 2.5ml spn
	salt and black pepper	

Garnish: 6 or 7 cutlet frills

6 or 7 glacé cherries, parsley sprigs

Cooking Temperature: 350°F, 180°C, Gas Mark 4

Method

1 **Fry** the onion and celery in the butter until soft.

2 **Mix** all the stuffing ingredients together and put into the prepared crown.

3 **Twist** small pieces of foil round the exposed bones of the crown to prevent charring.

4 **Brush** the crown with melted butter and sprinkle with lamb seasoning.

5 **Cook** for 1½-2 hours allowing 30 minutes per lb and 30 minutes extra.

6 **Remove** the foil and place cutlet frills and cherries on alternate bones.

7 **Place** on a serving dish and garnish with sprigs of parsley.

Duchesse

Ingredients		Serves 4
2oz	butter	50g
	salt and pepper	
	nutmeg	
1lb	British potatoes, cooked and sieved	450g
1	egg, size 3, yolk	1

Garnish: watercress

Method

1 **Beat** 1oz (25g) butter, seasoning and nutmeg into the potatoes.
2 **Place** the mixture in a saucepan, add the egg yolk and mix well on a low heat until the mixture leaves the base of the pan clean.
3 **Place** the mixture in a piping bag fitted with a vegetable star nozzle.
4 **Pipe** pyramid shapes on to a greased baking tray.
5 **Melt** the remaining butter and use to brush the shapes lightly. Brown under a grill or in the top of the oven.
6 **Serve** garnished with watercress.

Parmentier

Ingredients		Serves 4
1lb	British potatoes	450g
2oz	lard or	50g
3 tblspn	oil	3 × 15ml spn
	salt and pepper	
½oz	butter	15g

Garnish: parsley

Cooking Temperature: 375°F, 190°C, Gas Mark 5

Method

1 **Cut** the potatoes into ½" (1cm) cubes, wash well and drain.
2 **Shallow** fry in hot fat until coloured. Drain off excess fat, season and finish cooking in the oven for 15 minutes.
3 **When** cooked, toss in the butter and garnish with parsley.

Croquette

Ingredients		Serves 4
1lb	Duchesse mixture, cooled (see recipe above)	450g
1	egg, size 3,	1
2½fl oz	milk	75ml
1oz	plain flour	25g
4oz	breadcrumbs	125g
	Oil for deep fat frying	

Cooking Temperature: 375°F, 190°C

Method

1 **Divide** the Duchesse mixture into 2oz (50g) portions and mould into cork shapes.
2 **Mix** the egg and milk together. Roll the croquettes in flour, pass through the egg mixture then coat with breadcrumbs.
3 **Heat** the oil to 375°F, 190°C. Place the croquettes in a frying basket and deep fry until golden brown.
4 **Drain** and serve.

Byron

Ingredients		Serves 4
4 × 8oz	British potatoes, scrubbed and baked	4 × 225g
	salt and pepper	
	nutmeg	
2oz	butter	50g
	plain flour	
2½fl oz	milk	75ml
1oz	Cheddar cheese, grated	25g

Garnish: watercress

Method

1 **Cut** the baked potatoes in half, scoop out the flesh into a bowl.
2 **Season** the potatoes with salt, pepper and nutmeg and mix in the butter.
3 **Mould** into medallion shapes on a floured board.
4 **Place** on a baking sheet, brush over the tops with a little milk, sprinkle with grated cheese.
5 **Flash** under a hot grill and serve garnished with watercress.

Electric gong to summon diners at Victorian Cragside, Northumberland — the first house to be lit by hydro - electricity.

Pictured from left:
Duchesse, Parmentier, Croquette, Byron.

Beef Wellington

Ingredients		Serves 4
2 tblspn	oil	2 × 15ml spn
4 × 4oz	fillet steaks	4 × 125g
4oz	mushrooms, sliced	125g
1	onion, finely chopped	1
½ tspn	mixed herbs	1 × 2.5ml spn
	salt and black pepper	
12oz	British potatoes, sliced and parboiled	350g
1lb	puff pastry	450g
1	egg, size 3, beaten	1
Cooking Temperature: 400°F, 200°C, Gas Mark 6		

Method

1 **Heat** the oil and brown the steaks rapidly on both sides. Remove from the pan.

2 **Reduce** the heat and fry the mushrooms and onion until soft. Stir in the herbs and seasoning, then add the potato slices. Remove from the heat and allow to cool.

3 **Roll** out the pastry into a 16″ (40cm) square. Divide into 4.

4 **Place** a quarter of the vegetable mixture into the centre of each pastry square. Lay a fillet steak on top.

5 **Dampen** the edges of the pastry and fold over to make a parcel. Seal the edges well.

6 **Place** on a baking tray with the sealed edges underneath. Brush with beaten egg and bake for 30 minutes or until the pastry is golden brown and well risen.

Chicken à la Camber

Ingredients		Serves 4
4	chicken breast fillets	4
2oz	butter	50g
	salt and black pepper	
Duchesse Mixture		
1½lb	British potatoes, cooked and sieved	675g
2oz	butter	50g
1	egg, size 3	1
pinch	nutmeg	pinch
	salt and black pepper	
Sauce		
1oz	butter	25g
2 tspn	curry powder	2 × 5ml spn
6oz can	evaporated milk	170g can
4.9oz can	condensed chicken soup	140g can
3 tblspn	mayonnaise	3 × 15ml spn
2 tblspn	lemon juice	2 × 15ml spn
	salt and black pepper	
2oz	Cheddar cheese, grated	50g
Garnish: parsley		
Cooking Temperature: 400°F, 200°C, Gas Mark 6		

Method

1 **Place** the chicken breast fillets in a casserole dish with the butter and seasoning. Bake uncovered for 50 minutes.

2 **Make** the duchesse mixture by beating the butter, egg, nutmeg and seasoning into the sieved potato.

3 **Place** in a piping bag fitted with a vegetable star nozzle and pipe a border of potato round the edge of an oval serving dish. Flash under a hot grill until golden brown.

4 **Finally,** to make the sauce, melt the butter in a saucepan, add the curry powder and cook over a gentle heat for 2 minutes. Add the remaining ingredients except cheese and cook for 5 minutes, remove from the heat and stir in the cheese.

5 **Place** the chicken breast fillets in the centre of the serving dish and spoon over the sauce.

6 **Serve** garnished with parsley.

Crispy Beef Stroganoff

Ingredients		Serves 4
2lb	British potatoes, peeled and cut into ¾″ (2cm) dice	900g
1½lb	rump steak	675g
1oz	plain flour	25g
	salt and black pepper	
2oz	butter	50g
1 large	onion, finely chopped	1 large
8oz	mushrooms, sliced	225g
½pt	soured cream	300ml
2 tblspn	brandy	2 × 15ml spn
	oil, for deep fat frying	
Garnish: parsley, chopped		
Cooking Temperature: 375°F, 190°C		

Method

1 **Heat** the oil to 375°F, 190°C, and deep fry the diced potatoes for 2 minutes. Drain.

2 **Beat** the steak and cut into strips ¼″ × 2″ (5mm × 5cm). Coat with seasoned flour and fry in 1oz (25g) butter for 5-7 minutes. Remove from the pan.

3 **Fry** the onion and mushrooms in the remaining butter for 7 minutes. Add the steak and season to taste.

4 **Stir** the cream and brandy into the meat mixture and heat through but do not boil.

5 **Deep** fry the diced potatoes for a further 2 minutes or until golden brown in colour. Drain.

6 **Use** the potatoes to form a border round a heated serving platter.

7 **Pour** the beef stroganoff into the centre of the platter and garnish with chopped parsley.

The view of Snowdonia across the Menai Strait inspired Rex Whistler's amazing wall painting in the dining room at Plas Newydd, Anglesey.

Pictured from left:
Crispy Beef Stroganoff, Chicken à la Camber, Beef Wellington.

Pictured from left:
Creamy Bakes, Summer Puff, Cheese and Prawn Flans.

Summer Puff

Ingredients		Serves 4
1lb	frozen puff pastry, thawed	450g
1	egg, size 3, to glaze	1
1oz	butter	25g
1 medium	onion, chopped	1 medium
1oz	plain flour	25g
¼pt	white wine	150ml
¼pt	single cream	150ml
8oz	plaice, cooked and flaked	225g
8oz	British potatoes, diced and cooked	225g
2oz	peeled prawns	50g
2	tomatoes, skinned, de-seeded and chopped	2
1 tblspn	tomato purée	1 × 15ml spn
1 tblspn	fresh dill, chopped	1 × 15ml spn
1 tblspn	chives, chopped	1 × 15ml spn
	salt and black pepper	

Cooking Temperature: 400°F, 200°C, Gas Mark 6

Method

1 **Roll** out the pastry into an oblong shape, ¼" (5mm) thick. Run a pointed knife around the edge of the pastry to make a thin cut about ⅛" (3mm) in from the edge of the pastry.

2 **Make** diagonal slashes across the top of the lid of the pastry.

3 **Moisten** a baking sheet with a little water and place the pastry on it. Chill for 10 minutes.

4 **Brush** with beaten egg and cook until golden brown.

5 **To** make the filling, melt the butter and cook onion until transparent.

6 **Stir** in the flour. Cook for 2 minutes. Slowly add the wine and cream, stirring until smooth. Cook until thick.

7 **Add** the fish, potatoes, prawns, tomatoes, tomato purée, dill, chives and seasoning. Bring to the boil.

8 **Allow** the filling to cool. With a sharp knife, cut round and ease out the puff pastry lid.

9 **Gently** smooth the filling into the pastry case and replace the lid.

10 **Serve** chilled with a crisp green salad.

Creamy Bakes

Ingredients		Serves 4
4 × 8oz	British potatoes, scrubbed and baked	4 × 225g
8oz	full fat cream cheese	225g
3 tblspn	mayonnaise or	3 × 15ml spn
	yoghurt dressing	
½	red pepper, finely chopped	½
2 tspn	fresh chives, finely chopped	2 × 5ml spn
	salt and black pepper	
4	eggs, size 3, hard boiled and chopped	4

Garnish: red pepper and chives, finely chopped

Method

1 **Make** the filling by softening the cream cheese in a medium sized bowl.

2 **Beat** in the mayonnaise. Add the red pepper and chives and season. Fold in the hard boiled eggs.

3 **Make** a crosswise incision in the potatoes and open out by pressing at the base of the potatoes. Divide the filling between the hot potatoes.

4 **Garnish** each potato with red pepper and chives. Serve.

Cheese and Prawn Flans

Ingredients		Makes 6 small flans or 1 large
Pastry		
3oz	British potatoes, cooked and sieved	75g
6oz	plain flour	175g
1½oz	margarine	40g
1½oz	lard	40g
pinch	salt	pinch
Filling		
2oz	butter	50g
2oz	flour	50g
½pt	milk	300ml
	salt and black pepper	
1 tspn	tomato purée	1 × 5ml spn
6oz	British potatoes, diced and cooked	175g
6oz	prawns	175g
4oz	Cheddar cheese, grated	125g

Garnish: whole prawns

Cooking Temperature: 400°F, 200°C, Gas Mark 6

Method

1 **To** make the pastry, place all the ingredients in a bowl. Mix with a fork. Do not add water. Alternatively, a food processor can be used.

2 **Roll** out and line 6 × 3" (8cm) flan tins or an 8" (20cm) flan dish.

3 **Prick** the bases with a fork and bake for 15 minutes until the pastry is cooked. Remove from the oven.

4 **For** the filling, melt the butter in a saucepan, add the flour and heat for a further two minutes.

5 **Remove** from the heat and gradually add the milk.

6 **Return** to the heat, season and add the tomato purée, stirring. Once thickened, again remove from the heat, add the potato and prawns and half the cheese.

7 **Fill** the flan cases, sprinkle the remaining cheese over the flans and return to oven. Bake for 15-20 minutes, until the cheese has browned on top.

8 **Garnish** with whole prawns and serve.

Pictured from left:
Cheesy Caraway Rolls, Pizza and Bread Rolls.

Potato Dough

Ingredients

2 tspn	dried yeast	2 × 5ml spn
pinch	sugar	pinch
½pt	warm water	300ml
1lb	strong white flour	450g
2 tspn	salt	2 × 5ml spn
4oz	British potatoes, cooked and sieved	125g
	flour for kneading	

Method

1 **Sprinkle** the yeast and sugar onto the warm water. Stir and leave for about 10 minutes until it is frothy.
2 **Sieve** the flour and salt into a bowl and rub in the sieved potato.
3 **Stir** the yeast liquid into the flour and mix to form a dough.
4 **Turn** the dough onto a floured surface and knead until it is smooth, elastic and no longer sticky. This will take about 10 minutes.
5 **Place** the dough into an oiled polythene bag, or into a clean bowl, covering it with oiled cling film. Leave in a warm place for about an hour or until doubled in size.
6 **'Knock back'** the dough to its former volume and knead for about one minute.

Use as required in the recipes given.

Bread Rolls

Ingredients   Makes 16

1 quantity	potato dough	1 quantity
	milk or beaten egg to glaze	
	sesame seeds **or** poppy seeds	

Cooking Temperature: 450°F, 230°C, Gas Mark 8

Method

1 **Divide** the dough into 16 pieces weighing 2oz (50g) each.
2 **Shape** as required into rolls, plaits, cottage loaves or knots. Brush with milk or beaten egg and sprinkle with seeds if liked.
3 **Cover** and leave to prove for about 25 minutes.
4 **Bake** in a very hot oven for 15 minutes, or until the rolls sound hollow when tapped on the bottom.

Cheesy Caraway Rolls

Ingredients   Makes 8

1 quantity	potato dough	1 quantity
6oz	cheese, grated	175g
2 tspn	caraway seeds	2 × 5ml spn
	flour for dusting	

Cooking Temperature: 425°F, 220°C, Gas Mark 7

Method

1 **When** making the dough, add most of the cheese and the caraway seeds to the flour mixture before adding the yeast mixture. Proceed as in the basic method.
2 **Grease** a deep tin measuring approximately 7″ × 10″ (17.5cm × 25cm). Roll out the dough to fit the tin.
3 **Place** the dough in the tin and mark deeply with a knife into 8 pieces.
4 **Dust** well with flour and sprinkle with the remaining cheese. Leave to prove for about 30 minutes.
5 **Bake** for 30 minutes until well risen and brown.
6 **Eat** hot or cold with butter, cut into eight.

Pizza

Ingredients   Serves 4-6

Scone Base		
12oz	plain flour	350g
1 tspn	salt	1 × 5ml spn
2 tspn	baking powder	2 × 5ml spn
4oz	British potatoes, cooked and sieved	125g
3oz	margarine	75g
6fl oz	milk	180ml
Topping		
1	onion, sliced	1
1	green pepper, sliced	1
4oz	mushrooms, sliced	125g
1 tblspn	oil	1 × 15ml spn
1 tblspn	tomato purée	1 × 15ml spn
8oz can	tomatoes	227g can
1 tspn	pizza seasoning	1 × 5ml spn
1 tspn	basil	1 × 5ml spn
	salt and black pepper	
4oz	Cheddar cheese, grated	125g

Cooking Temperature: 425°F, 220°C, Gas Mark 7

Method

1 **Sieve** the flour, salt and baking powder into a bowl. Rub in the potatoes and margarine.
2 **Make** a well in the centre and add the milk slowly until the mixture forms a dough.
3 **Knead** for two minutes and roll onto a floured surface to make a 12″ (30cm) circle and place onto a greased baking tray.
4 **Fry** the onion, pepper and mushrooms in the oil until soft, add the tomato purée, tomatoes, pizza seasoning, basil, salt and pepper. Simmer for 5-10 minutes until the mixture has slightly thickened.
5 **Spread** the topping over the scone base and sprinkle with cheese.
6 **Bake** for 30 minutes until cheese is golden brown.
7 **Serve** hot or cold with a crisp salad.

Recipes with an Overseas Flavour

To have included a recipe from every country that uses potatoes would have required a book of enormous size and so in bringing to your kitchen a taste of foreign parts we have concentrated on dishes which reflect the cosmopolitan life of Britain today.

In Britain where Chinese, Indian and Greek takeaways and high class Italian and French restaurants are as familiar a sight in the High Street as Woolworths and Marks and Spencer. So in this chapter you will find dishes from India, Thailand, Switzerland to name but a few but wherever they come from they all have one thing in common — potatoes. For potatoes are the raison d'etre of this book and however far you travel in your kitchen it's nice to know British potatoes are always close at hand.

Stained glass window, side table and French Empire candelabra in the Service Lobby at Uppark, West Sussex.

Late-seventeenth century tin-glazed earthenware charger, decorated with the arms of the Weaver Company, at Cotehele House, Cornwall.

Blue and white theme on an old kitchen dresser at Saltram, Plymouth.

Pictured from left:
Swiss Rosti, Tandoori Oven Chips, Potato Fondue and
Chinese Style Beef.

Potato Fondue

Ingredients		Serves 4
1 clove	garlic	1 clove
¼pt	dry white wine	150ml
1 tblspn	cornflour	1 × 15ml spn
4oz	Emmenthal cheese, diced	125g
4oz	Gruyère cheese, diced	125g
pinch	nutmeg	pinch
1lb	British new potatoes, or small maincrop potatoes, cooked	450g

Method

1 **Rub** the inside of a saucepan with the garlic clove.

2 **Mix** 1 tblspn (1 × 15ml spn) of white wine with 1 tblspn (1 × 15ml spn) of cornflour. Reserve.

3 **Pour** the remaining wine into the prepared saucepan. Add the cheeses and nutmeg.

4 **Gradually** allow the cheeses to melt, stir in the cornflour mixture and bring to the boil.

5 **Pour** into a serving dish and place over a fondue burner if available. With long handled forks dip the potatoes into the fondue mixture and eat immediately.

Swiss Rosti

Ingredients		Serves 4
1½lb	British potatoes, peeled	675g
2oz	butter	50g
1	onion, finely chopped	1
dash	Worcestershire sauce	dash
	salt and black pepper	

Method

1 **Parboil** the potatoes for 7 minutes. Drain and allow to cool.

2 **Melt** the butter in a large frying pan and fry the onion.

3 **Grate** the potatoes and stir into the onion. Press flat, and cook until brown, approximately 7 minutes.

4 **Place** plate on top and invert. Slide back into pan and cook for a further 7 minutes to brown the other side.

Potato and Carrot Bourguignon

Ingredients		Serves 4-6
½oz	butter	15g
1 tblspn	oil	1 × 15ml spn
1lb	British potatoes cut into 1″ (2½cm) cubes	450g
8oz	carrots, peeled and cut into Julienne strips	225g
1	onion, chopped	1
1	green pepper, sliced thinly	1
1	red pepper, sliced thinly	1
4oz	mushrooms, sliced	125g
1 tblspn	flour	1 × 15ml spn
¼pt	red wine	150ml
¼pt	vegetable stock	150ml
	salt and black pepper	

Cooking Temperature: 375°F, 190°C, Gas Mark 5

Method

1 **Heat** the butter and oil in a large frying pan.

2 **Add** the potatoes, carrots, onion and peppers. Fry for 5 minutes or until the vegetables are softened. Add the mushrooms and cook for a further minute.

3 **Stir** in the flour and cook for 1 minute. Add wine, stock and seasoning.

4 **Transfer** to a casserole dish. Cover and cook for one hour or until the vegetables are tender.

Spanish Lamb Casserole

Ingredients		Serves 4
1½lb	boneless lamb, cubed	675g
2 tblspn	oil	2 × 15ml spn
10	black olives, optional	10
1lb	British potatoes, diced	450g
1	onion, sliced	1
2	carrots, thinly sliced	2
2 sticks	celery, sliced	2 sticks
1oz	flour	25g
1 tblspn	paprika pepper	1 × 15ml spn
1 tblspn	vinegar	1 × 15ml spn
2 tblspn	tomato purée	2 × 15ml spn
1	orange, rind and juice	1
2oz	sultanas	50g
½pt	stock	300ml
	salt and black pepper	

Cooking Temperature: 350°F, 180°C, Gas Mark 4

Method

1 **Brown** the lamb briskly in hot oil then remove to a casserole with the olives and the potatoes.

2 **In** the fat remaining in the pan gently fry the onion, carrots and celery for 3-4 minutes.

3 **Stir** in the flour, paprika, vinegar and tomato purée then add the rind and juice of the orange and the sultanas.

4 **Pour** in the stock stirring continuously until the mixture reaches boiling point. Season to taste.

5 **Transfer** the contents of the pan to the casserole. Cover and cook for 1½ hours.

Pictured from left:
Spanish Lamb Casserole, Potato Fondue, Swiss Rosti and
Potato and Carrot Bourguignon.

Pictured from left:
Chinese Style Beef, Chicken Bangkok and Chicken Oriental.

Chicken Bangkok

Ingredients

Serves 4

Topping

1	onion, chopped	1
1 small	red pepper, chopped	1 small
1lb	chicken breasts, cubed	450g
2 tblspn	oil	2 × 15ml spn
1oz	plain flour	25g
2 tspn	curry powder	2 × 5ml spn
¾pt	skimmed milk	450ml
1 tblspn	tomato purée	1 × 15ml spn
1 tblspn	fruit chutney	1 × 15ml spn
2oz	sultanas	50g
	salt and black pepper	

Potatoes

1½lb	British potatoes, sliced ⅛″ (3mm) thick and parboiled	675g
2 tspn	curry powder	2 × 5ml spn
3 tblspn	oil	3 × 15ml spn

Garnish: red pepper, chopped

Method

1 **Sauté** the onion, red pepper, reserving some for garnish and the chicken in the oil until the vegetables are soft. Stir in the flour and curry powder and continue cooking for 2-3 minutes.

2 **Gradually** pour in the milk, stirring continuously until the mixture comes to the boil.

3 **Add** the tomato purée, chutney and sultanas. Season to taste. Cover and simmer for 20-25 minutes or until the chicken is tender.

4 **Dust** the potato slices lightly with curry powder and sauté in hot oil for 10-15 minutes until golden brown.

5 **Arrange** the potato slices on the bottom of a shallow serving dish then pile the chicken mixture on top, leaving the outer ring of potato slices exposed.

6 **Garnish** with the remaining chopped red pepper and serve.

Chinese Style Beef

Ingredients

Serves 4

2 tblspn	oil	2 × 15ml spn
8oz	rump steak, cut into thin strips	225g
1	green pepper, thinly sliced	1
4oz	mushrooms, sliced	125g
12oz	British potatoes, grated	350g
1 tblspn	soy sauce	1 × 15ml spn
1 tspn	cumin	1 × 5ml spn
1 tblspn	demerara sugar	1 × 15ml spn
	salt and black pepper	
4oz	beansprouts	125g

Method

1 **Heat** the oil in a large frying pan or wok and sauté the steak until browned.

2 **Add** the pepper and mushrooms and fry until the mushrooms are soft. Then add the potatoes and fry for a further 5-10 minutes, stirring continuously.

3 **Stir** in the soy sauce, cumin, sugar and seasoning and fry for a further 5 minutes.

4 **Finally,** add the beansprouts, stir for 1 minute and serve immediately.

Oriental Chicken

Ingredients

Serves 4

1 tblspn	oil	1 × 15ml spn
1oz	butter	25g
12oz	chicken breasts	350g
14oz can	pineapple pieces	400g can
1lb	British potatoes, sliced and cooked	450g
½	red pepper, diced	½
½	green pepper, diced	½
4oz	mushrooms, sliced	125g
8oz	celery, thinly sliced	225g
1oz	cornflour	25g
2 tblspn	soy sauce	2 × 15ml spn
2 tblspn	clear honey	2 × 15ml spn
1 tblspn	vinegar	1 × 15ml spn
½ tspn	ground ginger	1 × 2.5ml spn
	salt and black pepper	

Garnish: salted cashew nuts

Method

1 **Heat** the oil and the butter in a large frying pan.

2 **Cut** the chicken into small cubes and fry for 5-10 minutes.

3 **Drain** and reserve the juice from the pineapple. Add the pineapple pieces and the remaining vegetables to the frying pan and fry briskly for 2 minutes.

4 **Blend** the cornflour with the pineapple juice, soy sauce, honey, vinegar, ginger and seasoning.

5 **Pour** over the chicken and vegetables and stir until the mixture comes to the boil and thickens slightly. Turn into a serving dish.

6 **Garnish** with salted cashew nuts and serve hot while the vegetables are still crunchy.

An interesting range, with separate roasting fire, in the kitchen at Brodick Castle, Isle of Arran.

Pictured from left:
Aloo Bonda, and Tandoori Oven Chips.

Aloo Bonda

Ingredients		Serves 4
4oz	plain flour	125g
pinch	salt	pinch
pinch	baking powder	pinch
½ tspn	chilli powder	1 × 2.5ml spn
¼pt	water	150ml
4 tblspn	mango chutney	4 × 15ml spn
½oz	ginger root, peeled and very finely chopped	15g
1	green chilli, de-seeded and finely chopped	1
1 small	onion, finely chopped	1 small
1lb	British potatoes, finely diced and cooked	450g
	oil for deep fat frying	

Cooking Temperature: 375°F, 190°C

Method

1 **Sift** the flour and salt with the baking powder and chilli powder.

2 **Gradually** add the water and mix well to make a smooth batter.

3 **Mix** the mango chutney, ginger root, chilli and onion into the batter mixture.

4 **Heat** the oil to 375°F, 190°C.

5 **Take** 1 tblspn (1 × 15ml spn) of potatoes and squeeze into a ball. Dip into the batter to coat and place into the fat and cook for about 3 minutes until golden brown. Repeat until all the potato has been used.

6 **Drain** well and serve hot.

Tandoori Oven Chips

Ingredients		Serves 4
2 tblspn	oil	2 × 15ml spn
2 cloves	garlic, crushed	2 cloves
1 tspn	Tandoori spice	1 × 5ml spn
1lb	British potatoes, scrubbed and cut into large chips	450g
	salt	

Cooking Temperature: 425°F, 220°C, Gas Mark 7

Method

1 **Mix** the oil, garlic and tandoori spice in a bowl.

2 **Add** the chips to the mixture and toss until thoroughly coated.

3 **Spread** on a baking sheet and bake for 30 minutes or until the chips are cooked.

4 **Sprinkle** with salt and serve hot.

A tempting table is depicted in this detail from one of the eighteenth century tapestries at Erddig, near Wrexham.

Summer Days

During the Summer delicious new potatoes are synonymous with the long hot days we all hope will come our way so in this section of our book we have chosen seven largely outdoor settings for each of the recipes with which you can use either new potatoes or small maincrop potatoes.

From this chapter you will see that all kinds of exciting recipes can be prepared using potatoes in dishes as different from Salad with Chicory to Kebabs with Spicy Tomato Sauce.

That latter dish is of course a MUST for those of you who enjoy barbecues.

Don't forget, for added fibre and goodness always serve British new potatoes in their skins, for there is a concentration of essential nutrients, including Vitamin C, just under the skin. To ensure that special flavour which only really fresh British new potatoes can provide buy them daily to benefit from the farmers' efforts in getting them to the shops within 24 hours of lifting.

Copper utensils gleam in the basement kitchen at Uppark, West Sussex.

The drawing room overlooking the Victorian gardens at Lanhydrock, near Bodmin.

Eighteenth century bouquet made of paper and wire flowers by lady's maid and companion, Elizabeth Ratcliffe, at Erddig, near Wrexham.

71

Pictured from left:
Curried Chicken Salad, Lily Potato Salad, Salmon and Leek
Quiche, Picnic Pie, Barbecued Potatoes.

Picnic Pie

Ingredients		Serves 4-6
Wholemeal Potato Pastry		
6oz	British potatoes, cooked and sieved	175g
6oz	plain flour	175g
6oz	wholemeal flour	175g
3oz	margarine	75g
3oz	lard	75g
pinch	salt	pinch
Filling		
8oz	bacon, chopped	225g
1 large	onion, finely chopped	1 large
1 tblspn	oil	1 × 15ml spn
1lb	British potatoes, sliced and cooked	450g
1	egg, size 3, beaten	1
3 tblspn	milk	3 × 15ml spn
	salt and black pepper	
6oz	Cheddar cheese, grated	175g

Cooking Temperature: 400°F, 200°C, Gas Mark 6

Method

1 **To make** the pastry, place all the ingredients in a bowl. Mix with a fork. Do not add water. Alternatively, a food processor can be used.

2 **Turn** out onto a floured surface and roll out two-thirds of the pastry to line a 9″ (23cm) flan dish.

3 **Fry** the bacon and onion in the oil until the onion is soft. Place into the prepared flan dish.

4 **Layer** the potatoes on top of the bacon and onion mixture.

5 **Beat** the egg and milk together and season. Pour over the potatoes, reserving a little for glazing the pie.

6 **Sprinkle** the cheese over the top and season once more.

7 **Roll** out the remaining pastry to form a lid. Dampen the edges and place over the pie, making sure that the pie is sealed.

8 **Brush** with the remaining egg mixture and bake for 40 minutes until golden brown.

9 **Serve** hot or cold with a salad.

Curried Chicken Salad

Ingredients		Serves 4
1lb	British new potatoes, or small maincrop potatoes, washed and cooked	450g
8oz	chicken, cooked and diced	225g
1	green apple, diced	1
1	red pepper, diced	1
1oz	sultanas	25g
5 tblspn	curried mayonnaise	5 × 15ml spn

Garnish: watercress

Method

1 **Allow** the potatoes to cool.

2 **Mix** all the ingredients together in a large bowl.

3 **Serve** garnished with watercress.

To make curried mayonnaise, add 2 tspn (2 × 5ml spn) of mild curry powder to 5 tblspn (5 × 15ml spn) of mayonnaise.

Cottage Cheese Pie

Ingredients		Serves 4-6
Pastry		
4oz	British potatoes, cooked and sieved	125g
8oz	plain flour	225g
2oz	margarine	50g
2oz	lard	50g
pinch	salt	pinch
Filling		
8oz	cottage cheese with chives	225g
8oz	Cheddar cheese, grated	225g
1 clove	garlic, crushed	1 clove
2	eggs, size 3	2
	salt and black pepper	
10oz	British potatoes, cooked and diced	275g

Cooking Temperature: 375°F, 190°C, Gas Mark 5

Method

1 **To make** the pastry, place all the ingredients in a bowl. Mix with a fork. Do not add water. Alternatively, a food processor can be used.

2 **Roll** out two-thirds of the pastry to line an 8″ (20cm) flan dish.

3 **Blend** together the two cheeses, garlic and the beaten egg (reserving a little for glazing). Season, then fold in the diced potato.

4 **Turn** this mixture into the pastry case.

5 **Roll** out the remaining pastry and use to cover the pie. Brush the top with the reserved egg to glaze.

6 **Bake** for 40 minutes until golden brown. Cool.

7 **Serve** cold with a crisp green salad.

This eighteenth century dolls' house was made for Sarah Lethieullier, future mistress of Uppark, West Sussex.

Pictured from left:
Picnic Pie, Cottage Cheese Pie and Curried Chicken Salad.

Prawn Buns

Ingredients		Makes 24
Choux Pastry		
½pt	water	300ml
4oz	butter	125g
5oz	plain flour	150g
pinch	salt	pinch
3oz	British potatoes, cooked and sieved	75g
4	eggs, size 3, beaten	4
Filling		
6oz	British potatoes, diced small and cooked	175g
6oz	prawns	175g
5 tblspn	mayonnaise	5 × 15ml spn
5oz	cucumber, diced small	150g
1½ tblspn	tomato ketchup	1.5 × 15ml spn

Garnish: lettuce leaves

Cooking Temperature: 425°F, 220°C, Gas Mark 7

Method

1 **Place** the water and butter in a saucepan. Heat gently until the butter melts, then bring to the boil.
2 **Remove** from the heat and quickly mix in the flour sieved with the salt.
3 **Add** the potato and beat until smooth. Leave to cool slightly.
4 **Gradually** beat in the eggs. Beat mixture thoroughly. Leave until cool.
5 **Place** the mixture in a piping bag, fitted with a ½" (1cm) plain nozzle.
6 **Pipe** 24 equal-sized balls onto a greased baking sheet.
7 **Bake** at 425°F, 220°C, Gas Mark 7 for 5 minutes. Reduce heat to 350°F, 180°C, Gas Mark 4 for a further 20 minutes. Make a small split in each bun and dry out in oven for 5 minutes. Remove from the oven and cool.
8 **Place** all the ingredients for the filling in a bowl and mix together.
9 **Carefully** spoon the mixture into the buns and serve on a bed of lettuce.

Potato and Tuna Cocktail

Ingredients		Serves 4
8oz	British new potatoes, or small maincrop potatoes, diced and cooked	225g
3½oz can	tuna in brine, drained and flaked	85g can
3	tomatoes, chopped	3
½	green pepper, chopped	½
½	red pepper, chopped	½
1 small	onion, grated	1 small
2 tblspn	mayonnaise	2 × 15ml spn
½	lettuce	½

Method

1 **Place** the potatoes, tuna, green and red pepper and onion in a bowl and stir in the mayonnaise.
2 **Shred** the lettuce and place in the bottom of 4 glass goblets.
3 **Spoon** the potato and tuna mixture on top.

Beansprout Salad

Ingredients		Serves 4
8oz	British potatoes, diced and cooked	225g
1lb	beansprouts	450g
8oz can	red kidney beans, drained	220g can
1 tblspn	onion, grated	1 × 15ml spn
2 tblspn	parsley, chopped	2 × 15ml spn
7oz can	sweetcorn, drained	198g can
5 tblspn	mayonnaise	5 × 15ml spn

Method

1 **Place** all the ingredients in a large bowl and mix gently but thoroughly.
2 **Chill** before serving.

Some of the kitchen equipment has seen many years' service at Wallington, Northumberland.

75

Pictured from left:
Beansprout Salad, Potato and Tuna Cocktail and Prawn Buns.

Pictured from left:
Salmon and Leek Quiche, Lily Potato Salad and
Mushroom Dip.

Salmon and Leek Quiche

Ingredients		Serves 8
Pastry		
5oz	British potatoes, cooked and sieved	150g
10oz	granary flour	275g
2½oz	margarine	65g
2½oz	lard	65g
pinch	salt	pinch
Filling		
2oz	butter	50g
1lb	leeks, chopped and washed	450g
2oz	plain flour	50g
¾pt	milk	450ml
1 tspn	mustard	1 × 5ml spn
15oz can	red salmon, drained and flaked	425g can
6oz	Cheddar cheese, grated	175g
2	eggs, size 3, yolks	2
	salt and black pepper	

Cooking Temperature: 400°F, 200°C, Gas Mark 6

Method

1 **To** make the pastry, place all the ingredients in a bowl. Mix with a fork. Do not add water. Alternatively, a food processor can be used.

2 **Line** a 10″ (25cm) flan case with the pastry and bake blind for 15 minutes.

3 **To** make the filling, melt the butter in a medium-sized saucepan and fry leeks until soft. Add the flour and remove from the heat.

Gradually blend in the milk, return to heat and bring to the boil, stirring continuously.

4 **Remove** from the heat and add the mustard, salmon and 4oz (125g) of the cheese and beat in the egg yolks.

5 **Allow** to cool and pour into the flan case.

6 **Sprinkle** the top with the remaining cheese and bake for 20 minutes until golden brown.

Lily Potato Salad

Ingredients		Serves 4
1lb	British potatoes, diced and cooked	450g
4	eggs, size 3, hard boiled and chopped	4
1	yellow pepper, cut into strips	1
6	spring onions, chopped	6
6 tblspn	mayonnaise	6 × 15ml spn
	salt and black pepper	
1 head	chicory	1 head
1	orange, sliced	1

Method

1 **Place** all the ingredients except chicory and orange into a mixing bowl and mix well. Season to taste.

2 **Mound** the salad into the centre of a round serving plate.

3 **Cut** the orange slices in half and arrange round the salad.

4 **Place** the chicory leaves over the orange slices allowing the orange to show through.

Mushroom Dip with Potatoes

Ingredients		
1 clove	garlic, crushed	1 clove
4oz	mushrooms, sliced	125g
½oz	butter	15g
8oz	cream cheese	225g
3 tblspn	mayonnaise	3 × 15ml spn
1 tspn	lemon juice	1 × 5ml spn
	salt and black pepper	
16	British new potatoes, or small maincrop potatoes, washed and cooked	16

Accompaniments: potato crisps, sticks of carrot, sticks of cucumber or sticks of celery

Method

1 **Fry** the garlic and mushrooms in the butter. Leave to cool and sieve or liquidise.

2 **Beat** the cream cheese thoroughly until soft and add the mayonnaise, lemon juice, mushroom mixture and seasoning.

3 **Pour** into a small bowl and place onto a large platter.

4 **Place** round the dip the potatoes, crisps and any of the vegetables listed above.

5 **This** can be served as a starter or as part of a buffet.

Sir Edwin Lutyens, the architect of Castle Drogo in Devon, designed this pestle and mortar for the scullery.

Pictured from left:
Kebabs with Barbecue Sauce, Barbecued Potatoes and
Smoky Salad.

Barbecued Potatoes

Ingredients		Serves 4
1lb	British new potatoes, or small maincrop potatoes, washed	450g
4 tblspn	clear honey	4 × 15ml spn
3 tblspn	soy sauce	3 × 15ml spn
3 tblspn	tomato ketchup	3 × 15ml spn
few drops	tabasco sauce	few drops
½ tspn	garlic purée	1 × 2.5ml spn
½ tspn	mustard powder	1 × 2.5ml spn
pinch	paprika	pinch
	salt and black pepper	
3 tblspn	orange juice	3 × 15ml spn
4 tblspn	wine vinegar	4 × 15ml spn

Cooking Temperature: 400°F, 200°C, Gas Mark 6

Method

1 **Place** the potatoes in a roasting tin.
2 **Mix** together all the remaining ingredients and pour over the potatoes.
3 **Bake** the potatoes in the oven for 1¼ hours, turning once or twice in the sauce while cooking.

Smoky Salad

Ingredients		Serves 4
1lb	British potatoes or small maincrop potatoes, washed and cooked	450g
8oz	smoked trout, flaked	225g
4oz	mushrooms, sliced	125g
6	spring onions, chopped	6
¼pt	soured cream	150ml
2 tspn	horseradish sauce	2 × 5ml spn
3 tblspn	mayonnaise	3 × 15ml spn
	salt and black pepper	

Garnish: parsley

Method

1 **Allow** the potatoes to cool.
2 **Mix** the potatoes, trout, mushrooms and spring onions together.
3 **Mix** the soured cream, horseradish sauce and mayonnaise together, season and pour over the salad ingredients. Stir well.
4 **Serve** chilled, garnished with parsley.

Kebabs with Barbecue Sauce

Ingredients		Serves 4
Kebabs		
8 rashers	streaky bacon	8 rashers
12	British new potatoes or small maincrop potatoes, washed and parboiled	12
8	button mushrooms	8
1 small	green pepper, chopped	1 small
1 small	red pepper, chopped	1 small
1oz	butter, melted, to glaze	25g
Barbecue Sauce		
1 large	onion, finely chopped	1 large
4 tblspn	oil	4 × 15ml spn
2 tblspn	tomato purée	2 × 15ml spn
4oz	soft brown sugar	125g
2 tblspn	wine vinegar	2 × 15ml spn
few drops	chilli sauce	few drops
4 tspn	cornflour	4 × 5ml spn
¾pt	water	450ml
pinch	salt	pinch

Cooking Temperature: 400°F, 200°C, Gas Mark 6

Method

1 **Stretch** the bacon rashers with the back of a knife and roll up.
2 **Place** all the kebab ingredients alternately onto four skewers. Brush with butter and put onto a baking sheet.
3 **Cook** in the oven for 40 minutes, turning occasionally until cooked.
4 **To** make the sauce, fry the onion in the oil until soft.
5 **Add** the tomato purée, sugar, vinegar and chilli sauce. Stir well and remove from heat.
6 **Blend** the cornflour with a little of the water and gradually add to the onion mixture, add the remaining water. Return to the heat and bring to the boil stirring continuously. Season.
7 **Place** the kebabs on a serving dish and carefully spoon the sauce over them. Serve immediately.

This napkin press at Castle Drogo, Devon, was once used to provide immaculate table linen for meal times.

Cakes and Desserts
The 'Sweet' Potato

Few people realise that potatoes can be used to bring a whole new taste and texture to the kind of food least associated with them, namely desserts and cakes. For potatoes actually help to make these more moist, easier to slice, and longer lasting and nowhere is this better illustrated than in our recipes for Pineapple Upside Down Pudding and Special Chocolate Cake. Remember also that by using potatoes you will actually be adding essential nutrients which otherwise would not be present. So the appetising recipes in this chapter should tempt every cook who fancies trying her hand at something a little different. But beware! once you've made your cakes and desserts this way you probably won't want to make them any other way again. Finally, a tip — when the recipe calls for the potato to be mashed and sieved you will get an even better result if the potato is cold.

Ready-to-use kitchen utensils at Drum Castle, near Aberdeen.

Teatime in miniature in the parlour of the renowned eighteenth century dolls' house at Uppark, West Sussex.

The dairy at Uppark, West Sussex, where the mother of H.G. Wells was once housekeeper.

81

Pictured from left:
Pineapple Upside Down Pudding, Nutty Cherry Squares,
Jam Doughnuts, Chocolate Profiteroles and
Special Chocolate Cake.

Pictured from left:
Chocolate Pudding, Raspberry Mousse and
Pineapple Upside Down Pudding.

Raspberry Mousse

Ingredients		Serves 4
1lb	raspberries	450g
2oz	British potatoes, cooked and sieved	50g
1 tspn	lemon juice	1 × 5ml spn
2oz	caster sugar	50g
3 tspn	gelatine	3 × 5ml spn
2 tblspn	boiling water	2 × 15ml spn
½pt	double cream	300ml
2	eggs, size 3, whites	2
To decorate: whipped cream		
	raspberries	

Method

1 **Purée** the raspberries through a sieve into a bowl.

2 **Add** the potatoes, lemon juice and sugar.

3 **Dissolve** the gelatine in the water, cool slightly and whisk into the fruit purée.

4 **Whip** the cream until thick and stir into the mixture.

5 **Whisk** the egg whites until stiff and fold into the mousse. Chill for 1-2 hours.

6 **Decorate** with whipped cream and raspberries.

Pineapple Upside Down Pudding

Ingredients		Serves 4 6
2 tblspn	golden syrup, warmed	2 × 15ml spn
7¾oz can	pineapple slices and juice	220g can
4	glacé cherries, halved	4
6oz	soft margarine	175g
6oz	caster sugar	175g
4oz	British potatoes, cooked and sieved	125g
2	eggs, size 3, beaten	2
6oz	self-raising flour	175g

Cooking Temperature: 350°F, 180°C, Gas Mark 4

Method

1 **Grease** thoroughly a 7" (18cm) round cake tin.

2 **Pour** the golden syrup into the base of the tin and arrange the pineapple slices and cherries on the syrup.

3 **Beat** together the margarine, sugar and potatoes until light and fluffy.

4 **Gradually** beat in the eggs and fold in the flour.

5 **Carefully** stir in the pineapple juice until it forms a soft consistency.

6 **Pour** over the pineapple, smooth flat and bake in the oven for 1 hour 5 minutes. Once the top is golden brown, cover with foil.

7 **Remove** from oven, turn out onto a flat plate and serve hot with cream or custard.

Chocolate Pudding

Ingredients		Serves 4
Pudding		
4oz	British potatoes, cooked and sieved	125g
4oz	caster sugar	125g
4oz	margarine	125g
2oz	plain chocolate	50g
1 tblspn	milk	1 × 15ml spn
2	eggs, size 3, beaten	2
4oz	self-raising flour	125g
½oz	cocoa	15g
½oz	cornflour	15g
pinch	salt	pinch
Sauce		
1½ tblspn	cornflour	1.5 × 15ml spn
½pt	milk	300ml
2oz	plain chocolate, grated	50g
1 tspn	vanilla essence	1 × 5ml spn
½oz	butter	15g
2 tblspn	caster sugar	2 × 15ml spn

Method

1 **To make the pudding,** beat together the potatoes, sugar and margarine until light and fluffy.

2 **Melt** the chocolate with the milk in a bowl over a saucepan of hot water. Beat into the creamed mixture followed by the eggs.

3 **Sieve** together the flour, cocoa, cornflour and salt and fold in.

4 **Place** in a well greased 2pt (1.2 ltr) pudding bowl.

5 **Cover** securely with greaseproof paper or foil and steam for 1½ hours.

6 **To make the sauce,** mix cornflour with a little cold milk.

7 **Pour** remaining milk into a saucepan and add chocolate. Heat very slowly until chocolate melts.

8 **Pour** in the cornflour and mix well.

9 **Cook,** stirring continuously until sauce comes to the boil and thickens.

10 **Add** vanilla essence, butter and sugar and simmer for 3 minutes.

11 **To serve,** turn the pudding out onto a flat plate, pour over some of the sauce and serve the remainder in a sauce boat.

Below stairs in the early nineteenth century kitchen at Clandon Park, near Guildford, Surrey.

Chocolate and Orange Log

Ingredients		Serves 8
Cake		
3oz	British potatoes, cooked and sieved	75g
4oz	soft margarine	125g
6oz	caster sugar	175g
3	eggs, size 3, beaten	3
6oz	self-raising flour	175g
1 tspn	baking powder	1 × 5ml spn
2 tblspn	milk	2 × 15ml spn
½ tspn	orange rind, finely grated	1 × 2.5ml spn
few drops	orange food colouring	few drops
½oz	cocoa	15g
Filling		
2	oranges, segmented	2
3 tblspn	orange liqueur	3 × 15ml spn
2oz	British potatoes, cooked and sieved	50g
2oz	butter or margarine	50g
4oz	icing sugar, sieved	125g
1oz	cocoa, sieved	25g
Decoration		
½pt	double cream, whipped	300ml
2oz	plain chocolate, melted	50g

Cooking Temperature: 350°F, 180°C, Gas Mark 4

Method

1 To make the cake, place the potato, margarine, sugar, eggs, flour, baking powder and milk in a mixing bowl and beat, preferably with an electric whisk, until light and fluffy.

2 **Divide** the mixture in half. Add the orange rind and colouring to one half and the cocoa, mixed with a little hot water, to the other.

3 **Place** alternate spoonfuls of the mixture into a greased and lined 7″ × 11″ (17.5cm × 27.5cm) Swiss roll tin, to give a marbled effect. Bake for 25-30 minutes. Turn onto a wire cake rack to cool.

4 **When** the cake is cool, cut it in half lengthways then slice each half horizontally, so there are 4 long pieces of sponge.

5 **Soak** the orange segments in liqueur. Make the filling by creaming the potato and butter together and gradually beating in the icing sugar and cocoa.

6 **Sandwich** the layers of cake together with orange segments and filling. Spoon any excess liqueur over the top. Place on a serving dish.

7 **Cover** the log with whipped cream. Place the melted chocolate in a greaseproof paper piping bag and "dribble" it over the log.

Crispy Apple Pudding

Ingredients		Serves 4
3oz	butter	75g
6oz	self-raising flour	175g
6oz	soft brown sugar	175g
5 tblspn	milk	5 × 15ml spn
1	egg, size 3, beaten	1
3oz	British potatoes, cooked and sieved	75g
½	cooking apple, finely diced	½
½	cooking apple, thinly sliced	½
3oz	almonds, chopped	75g
2oz	butter, melted	50g

Cooking Temperature: 400°F, 200°C, Gas Mark 6

Method

1 **Rub** the butter into the flour, add 3oz (75g) of sugar and mix thoroughly.

2 **Pour** the milk into the beaten egg and add to the mixture, followed by the potatoes and diced apple and beat until all ingredients are combined.

3 **Put** the cake mixture into an 8″ (20cm) flan dish, arrange the sliced apple around the edge of the dish.

4 **Mix** together the remaining sugar, almonds, melted butter and spread over the top of the cake.

5 **Bake** for 35-40 minutes or until slightly risen and golden brown.

6 **Serve** hot with cream.

Sinks and plate drying racks designed by Sir Edwin Lutyens line a scullery wall at Castle Drogo.

85

Pictured from left:
Crispy Apple Pudding, Chocolate and Orange Log.

86

Pictured from left:
Three Kings Christmas Pudding, Orange Sandwich Cake and
Chocolate Profiteroles.

Chocolate Profiteroles

Ingredients
Makes 40

Choux Pastry

½pt	water	300ml
4oz	butter	125g
5oz	plain flour, sieved	150g
pinch	salt	pinch
3oz	British potatoes, cooked and sieved	75g
4	eggs, size 3, beaten	4

Filling

¾pt	double cream, whipped	450ml

Chocolate Sauce

4oz	chocolate, broken into pieces	125g
¼pt	single cream	150ml
2oz	butter, diced	50g
2	eggs, size 3, yolks	2
2 tblspn	Brandy (optional)	2 × 15ml spn

Cooking Temperature: 425°F, 220°C, Gas Mark 7

Method

1 **Place** the water and butter in a saucepan. Heat gently until the butter melts, then bring to the boil.
2 **Remove** from the heat and quickly mix in the flour and salt.
3 **Add** the potato and beat until smooth. Leave to cool slightly.
4 **Gradually** beat in the eggs, beat the mixture thoroughly and leave until cold.
5 **Place** the mixture in a piping bag, fitted with a ½" (1cm) plain nozzle.
6 **Pipe** 40 equal-sized balls onto greased baking sheets.
7 **Bake** in a pre-heated oven for 5 minutes at 425°F, 220°C, Gas Mark 7, then reduce the heat to 350°F, 180°C,

Gas Mark 4 for 20 minutes. Make a small slit in each bun and cook for a further 5 minutes. Remove from oven and place on a cooling rack.
8 **To** make the sauce, place the chocolate and cream in a bowl and melt the chocolate gently over a pan of hot water.
9 **Remove** from the heat and stir in the butter.
10 **Add** the remaining ingredients and beat until smooth.
11 **Pipe** the whipped cream into the choux buns and pile them onto a plate pyramid fashion.
12 **Pour** the warm chocolate sauce over the pyramid and serve.

Orange Sandwich Cake

Ingredients

4oz	soft margarine	125g
4oz	soft brown sugar	125g
2	oranges, juice and rind	2
2oz	carrot, grated	50g
2	eggs, size 3, beaten	2
6oz	British potatoes, cooked and sieved	175g
8oz	self-raising flour	225g
2 tspn	baking powder	2 × 5ml spn
1 tspn	cinnamon	1 × 5ml spn
1 tspn	ground ginger	1 × 5ml spn
2oz	sultanas	50g

Butter Cream

2oz	butter	50g
4oz	icing sugar	125g
1	orange, rind	1

Icing

4oz	icing sugar	125g
1	orange, juice	1

Garnish: crystallised orange pieces

Cooking Temperature: 325°F, 160°C, Gas Mark 3

Method

1 **Cream** together the margarine, sugar and the grated rind of two oranges.
2 **Stir** in the grated carrot.
3 **Gradually** beat the eggs into the creamed mixture.
4 **Fold** in the sieved potato, flour, baking powder, cinnamon, ginger and sultanas.
5 **Stir** in 4 tblspn (4 × 15ml spn) orange juice to give a soft mixture, add more if necessary.
6 **Divide** the mixture between two greased and lined 8" (20cm) sandwich tins.
7 **Bake** for 30 minutes.
8 **Make** the butter cream by beating together the butter, icing sugar and orange rind.
9 **Make** the icing by gradually adding the orange juice to the icing sugar so that the icing is of a coating consistency but not runny.
10 **When** the cakes are cool, sandwich together with butter cream and pour icing over the top, decorate with crystallised orange pieces.

Three Kings Christmas Pudding

Ingredients

1oz	ground almonds	25g
3oz	British potatoes, peeled and grated	75g
4oz	raisins	125g
4oz	sultanas	125g
4oz	currants	125g
3oz	carrot, grated	75g
3oz	apple, peeled and grated	75g
3oz	suet	75g
3oz	soft brown sugar	75g
3oz	self-raising flour	75g
3oz	fresh white breadcrumbs	75g
2oz	mixed peel	50g
1	egg, size 3	1
1 tblspn	black treacle	1 × 15ml spn
3 tblspn	Brandy or Rum	3 × 15ml spn
1 tspn	mixed spice	1 × 5ml spn
½ tspn	salt	1 × 2.5ml spn

Method

1 **In** a large mixing bowl combine all the ingredients until thoroughly mixed.
2 **Place** the mixture into a greased 2pt (1.2ltr) pudding basin.
3 **Cover** tightly with greaseproof paper and steam for 6 hours.
4 **Once** the pudding is cooked, it can be reheated by steaming for 2-4 hours.

Cakes and Desserts

Pictured from left:
Potato and Apple Scones, Apple and Banana Cakes, Special
Chocolate Cake.

Potato and Apple Scones

Ingredients   Makes 12

2oz	butter	50g
3oz	British potatoes, cooked and sieved	75g
6oz	self-raising flour, sieved	175g
2oz	caster sugar	50g
1	apple, finely grated and well drained	1
2 tblspn	honey	2 × 15ml spn
	sesame seeds	

Cooking Temperature: 400°F, 200°C, Gas Mark 6

Method

1 **Rub** the butter into the potatoes and flour until it resembles breadcrumbs.
2 **Stir** in the sugar and the apple.
3 **With** a fork, bring the ingredients together to form a soft dough.
4 **Turn** out onto a floured surface and knead for 1 minute until the dough is smooth.
5 **Roll** out to ½" (1cm) thick and cut into circles using a 2" (5cm) pastry cutter.
6 **Place** on a greased baking tray and cook for 20 minutes. Cool on a wire rack.
7 **Heat** the honey in a saucepan and brush the scones. Sprinkle with some sesame seeds.
8 **Serve** halved, spread with butter.

Special Chocolate Cake

Ingredients

Cake

4oz	British potatoes, cooked and sieved	125g
6oz	butter	175g
8oz	soft dark brown sugar	225g
3	eggs, size 3, beaten	3
3oz	plain chocolate, melted	75g
½ tspn	cinnamon	1 × 2.5ml spn
¼ tspn	nutmeg	½ × 2.5ml spn
8oz	self-raising flour, sieved	225g
1oz	cocoa, sieved	25g
2oz	walnuts, roughly chopped	50g

Filling

6 tblspn	marmalade	6 × 15ml spn

Icing

7oz	plain chocolate	200g
3oz	butter	75g
3	eggs, size 3, yolks	3
7oz	icing sugar, sieved	200g
2 tblspn	milk	2 × 15ml spn

Cooking Temperature: 350°F, 180°C, Gas Mark 4

Method

1 **Cream** the potato, butter and sugar until light and fluffy.
2 **Gradually** beat in the eggs.
3 **Stir** in the melted chocolate, cinnamon and nutmeg.
4 **Fold** in the flour, cocoa and walnuts.
5 **Divide** the mixture evenly between 2 × 8" (20cm) greased and lined sandwich tins. Bake for 30 minutes or until the sponge springs back to touch. Allow to cool and turn out.
6 **Allow** the marmalade to melt in a saucepan over a low heat. Sieve the marmalade and use half to sandwich the cakes together.
7 **With** a skewer, pierce holes through the cake, from the top to three-quarters down. Carefully pour the remaining marmalade into these holes.
8 **Gradually** melt the chocolate and butter together in a bowl over a pan of hot water. Allow to cool slightly.
9 **Beat** in the egg yolks and gradually mix in the icing sugar and milk. Coat the cake, top and sides, with the fudge icing.
10 **Once** the icing has set, the cake can be served. Do not store in the refrigerator.

Apple and Banana Cakes

Ingredients   Makes 12

Pastry

2oz	British potatoes, cooked and sieved	50g
4oz	plain flour	125g
1oz	margarine	25g
1oz	lard	25g
pinch	salt	pinch

Filling

4oz	British potatoes, cooked and sieved	125g
½	banana, mashed	½
1	egg, size 3, separated	1
1oz	caster sugar	25g
pinch	nutmeg	pinch
¼ tspn	cinnamon	½ × 2.5ml spn
1	lemon, juice and rind	1
1	cooking apple, finely chopped	1
2oz	icing sugar	50g

Cooking Temperature: 400°F, 200°C, Gas Mark 6

Method

1 **To** make the pastry, place all the ingredients in a bowl. Mix with a fork. Do not add water. Alternatively, a food processor can be used.
2 **Turn** onto a floured board and roll out to ¼" (5mm) thick. Using a pastry cutter, cut out 12 rounds and line a 12-hole bun tin.
3 **In** a bowl mix together the potato, banana, egg, caster sugar, nutmeg, cinnamon, lemon juice and rind.
4 **Whisk** the egg white stiffly and fold into the mixture. Spoon into pastry cases.
5 **Sprinkle** the apple over each filled pastry case and bake for 25 minutes. Allow to cool slightly and transfer to a cooling rack.
6 **When** cool, sprinkle with icing sugar and serve.

Nutty Cherry Squares

Ingredients		Makes 24
Base		
4oz	British potatoes, cooked and sieved	125g
5oz	margarine	150g
2½oz	soft brown sugar	65g
½ tspn	almond essence	1 × 2.5ml spn
4oz	glacé cherries, chopped	125g
7oz	plain flour	200g
Topping		
12oz	icing sugar, sieved	350g
3-4 tblspn	water	3-4 × 15ml spn
1oz	nibbed almonds	25g

Cooking Temperature: 350°F, 180°C, Gas Mark 4

Method

1 **Cream** together the potatoes, margarine and sugar until light and fluffy.

2 **Mix** in the almond essence and cherries followed by the flour.

3 **Put** the mixture into a greased and floured 7″ × 11″ (17.5cm × 27.5cm) Swiss roll tin.

4 **Bake** for 30 minutes until light golden brown. Remove from oven and cool in the tin.

5 **Put** the icing sugar into a bowl and gradually stir in the water. Stir until smooth and glossy.

6 **Pour** over the cooled cake and sprinkle with almonds. Cut into 24 squares and serve.

Currant and Peanut Biscuits

Ingredients		Makes 20-25
3oz	British potatoes, cooked and sieved	75g
4oz	margarine	125g
4oz	soft brown sugar	125g
6oz	plain flour	175g
½ tspn	cinnamon	1 × 2.5ml spn
2oz	salted peanuts	50g
2oz	currants	50g

Cooking Temperature: 350°F, 180°C, Gas Mark 4

Method

1 **Cream** together the potato, margarine and sugar until light and fluffy.

2 **Fold** in the other ingredients and mix thoroughly.

3 **Place** in refrigerator for 20 minutes.

4 **Turn** the dough onto a floured surface and roll to ¼″ (5mm) thick. Cut out the biscuits with a 2¾″ (7cm) fluted cutter.

5 **Place** on a greased baking tray and bake for 15 minutes until golden brown.

6 **Allow** the biscuits to cool slightly then transfer to a cooling rack.

Jam Doughnuts

Ingredients		Makes 16
½oz	fresh yeast **or**	15g
1½ tspn	dried yeast	1.5 × 5ml spn
1 tspn	caster sugar	1 × 5ml spn
8fl oz	warm milk	240ml
1lb	strong white flour	450g
1 tspn	salt	1 × 5ml spn
2oz	butter	50g
4oz	British potatoes, cooked and sieved	125g
1	egg, size 3, beaten	1
	oil for deep fat frying	
4oz	caster sugar	125g
	jam	

Cooking Temperature: 350°F, 180°C.

Method

1 **Place** the fresh yeast in a jug with the sugar and a little of the warm milk. Stir thoroughly, then add remaining milk gradually.

2 **When** using dried yeast, sprinkle it with the caster sugar onto the warm milk and follow instructions on the packet.

3 **Sieve** the flour and salt into a mixing bowl. Rub in the butter.

4 **Stir** in the potato, yeast mixture and beaten egg, mixing well until a smooth dough is formed.

5 **Turn** the dough onto a floured surface and knead for 10 minutes or until dough is smooth and elastic.

6 **Place** the dough in a lightly floured bowl and leave, covered with oiled cling film, in a warm place for 40-45 minutes, or until dough has doubled in size.

7 **'Knock back'** the dough and knead for a further 2-3 minutes. Divide evenly into 16 pieces and shape each piece quickly into a smooth ball.

8 **Place** on a greased baking sheet (well spaced out), cover again and leave for 20 minutes.

9 **Heat** the oil to 350°F, 180°C.

10 **Carefully** lower 3 or 4 doughnuts into the oil and cook for 4 minutes, making sure to turn during cooking. Drain well. Repeat for remaining doughnuts.

11 **In** a bag, place the caster sugar and toss each doughnut so that it is evenly coated.

12 **Make** a small hole in the side of each doughnut with a knife.

13 **Using** a small teaspoon or piping bag fitted with a plain nozzle, place the jam into each doughnut.

Waste lemon skins dipped in salt and silver sand were used to clean the copper utensils to be seen at Brodie Castle, Morayshire.

Pictured from left:
Currant and Peanut Biscuits, Jam Doughnuts and
Nutty Cherry Squares.

Potatoes as an Accompaniment

Whether boiled, mashed, roast or chipped, good potatoes can be spoiled by poor preparation.

Follow these hints and recipes for the best results.

Potatoes require gentle cooking in only enough water to cover. The cooking water can be used for gravy, soup or sauce.

For **Potatoes** that tend to discolour after boiling add 1 dessertspoonful of vinegar or lemon juice to every pint of water 10 minutes before the end of cooking.

Potatoes pressure cooked, especially in their skins, retain more of the Vitamin C content.

Potatoes should be served immediately to preserve the Vitamin C.

Chipped Potatoes

1lb	potatoes	450g
	oil or lard	

Method

1 **Cut** the potatoes into ½" (1cm) fingers and place in a bowl of ice cold water for about 10 minutes.
2 **Drain** and dry thoroughly.
3 **Place** the fat into a deep pan (you will require 1½ pints (900ml) of oil for ½lb (225g) chips in an 8" (20cm) standard chip pan) and heat to 375°F, 190°C or until a piece of bread will brown on one side in 30 seconds.
4 **Place** the chips into a frying basket and lower gently into the oil and cook for 3 minutes.
5 **Remove** basket and allow the fat to reheat to 375°F, 190°C and cook the chips for a further 5 minutes until crisp and golden brown.

Boiled Potatoes

1lb	potatoes, peeled	450g
1 tspn	salt	1 × 5ml spn
	water	

Method

1 **Place** the potatoes and salt into a pan and barely cover with cold water.
2 **Place** the lid on the pan and bring to the boil.
3 **Reduce** the heat and simmer the potatoes until cooked.
4 **Drain** and dry over a low heat with the lid of the pan tilted.

Mashed Potatoes

1lb	potatoes, boiled	450g
1oz	butter	25g
1 tblspn	hot milk	1 × 15ml spn
	pepper	

Method

1 **Add** the butter and milk to the potatoes.
2 **Mash** thoroughly and season with pepper.

Roast Potatoes

1lb	potatoes, peeled	450g
	salt and pepper	
	oil or fat	

Method

1 **Cut** potatoes into even sized pieces, and parboil for 10 minutes. Drain and dry.
2 **Pour** sufficient oil or fat into a roasting pan and place in the oven to heat the fat.
3 **Remove** and add the dry potatoes, dust with salt and pepper.
4 **Return** to the oven and cook at 425°F, 220°C, Gas Mark 7, basting occasionally with the fat until cooked, crisp and golden. Drain.

Boiled New Potatoes

1lb	potatoes, scrubbed or scraped	450g
1 tspn	salt	1 × 5ml spn
	boiling water	

Method

1 **Place** the potatoes and salt into a pan and barely cover with boiling water.
2 **Place** the lid on the pan and boil gently until cooked, 15-20 minutes according to size.
3 **Drain** well. Toss in butter if desired.

Sauté Potatoes

1lb	potatoes	450g
2oz	butter or oil	50g

Method

1 **Peel** the potatoes thinly and parboil in salted water for about 10 minutes.
2 **Drain** well and dry off in the pan over a low heat.
3 **Cut** the potatoes into ¼" (5mm) thick slices.
4 **Heat** the butter or cooking oil in a frying pan, add the potatoes and fry on both sides until crisp and brown. (Approximately 10 minutes).

Helpful Hints

- Treat potatoes with care.
  They bruise easily

- Remove potatoes from polythene bags.
  This avoids sweating

- Keep potatoes in the dark.
  Light turns them green

- Peel potatoes thinly.
  To preserve nutrients just under the skin

- Cut potatoes into equal-sized pieces.
  To ensure even cooking

- Boil potatoes slowly.
  To avoid them breaking down

- Add lemon juice during boiling.
  To avoid after-cooking blackening

- Save the water used for cooking potatoes.
  To use for soups, gravies and sauces.

- Don't try mashing potatoes in a food
  processor. They will become very runny

- If you own a microwave oven you can
  easily use it to cook sliced potato for use
  as a topping or in layered dishes.
  Place the slices in a bowl and add
  water. Cover and cook. They will only
  take a few minutes

- Cook diced potato and serve hot, tossed
  in butter and freshly chopped herbs.
  This makes an unusual border for main
  course dishes

- If you are a flower arranger, use half a
  large potato as a base for woody stems
  instead of a piece of oasis. This is really
  useful at Christmas time for holly

- Sauté flaked almonds in butter.
  Add a little lemon juice then immediately
  pour over boiled potatoes to give a mouth
  watering topping

- For a crunchy topping, keep some
  toasted sesame seeds in an airtight
  container and use to sprinkle onto cooked
  potatoes.
  They give a crunchy texture, nutty flavour
  and attractive appearance.

- Chopped herbs, loosely packed in plastic
  containers and frozen can be used straight
  from the freezer to garnish all kinds of
  potato dishes at the last minute

- Add a touch of ground nutmeg to
  mashed potato, it makes a surprising
  difference to the flavour.

Cookery Demonstrations

If you are interested in learning more
about potatoes by means of a cookery
demonstration, one of our Home
Economists will be pleased to come along
and visit your group.

We do prefer to have at least 40 people
attending the demonstration.

For further details contact:

England and Wales
Janet Cooke,
Potato Marketing Board,
50 Hans Crescent, Knightsbridge,
London SW1X 0NB
Telephone: 01-589 4874

Scotland
Potato Marketing Board,
Cookery Demonstration Service,
8 Manor Place, Edinburgh EH3 7DD
Telephone: 031-225 1466

A

B

C

D

F

H

J

K

Why Not Join The National Trust?

It costs the National Trust many millions of pounds a year to care for all the countryside, coast, gardens and historic buildings which it owns in England, Wales and Northern Ireland. As an independent charity, it receives no regular Government subsidy: the subscriptions of its members therefore make a vital contribution to the conservation of our natural and architectural heritage.

Members are admitted free to some 250 properties for which there is normally an entrance charge. They also receive a copy of the annual handbook which gives details of those properties and their opening times, plus a regular colour magazine.

The Trust has several types of membership, including family group, which offers free admission to both adults and their children, a special rate for those under 23, life membership and corporate membership for schools. National Trust membership also makes a perfect gift.

For further details write to:
The National Trust Membership Dept., P.O. Box 39, Bromley, Kent BR1 1NH.

For details about membership of The National Trust for Scotland, write to its head office at: 5 Charlotte Square, Edinburgh EH2 4DU.

Acknowledgements

The assistance provided by the National Trust and the National Trust for Scotland was considerable in the preparation of this recipe book. In particular we wish to thank the staff at 36 Queen Anne's Gate, London, SW1H 9AS and 5 Charlotte Square, Edinburgh, EH2 4DU for the loan of their library photographs used in this book. These photographs were taken by: *J. Batty, John Bethell, A.C. Cooper, David Cripps, Mike Henton, Sheila Orme, Erik Pelham, Joe Rock, Tim Stephens, Charlie Waite, Jeremy Whitaker.* The line drawing on page 6 is by *Claude Page.*

All photographs of the actual dishes are by *David Warne* and, with the exception of those on pages 19, 23, 26, 40, 46, 51, 52, 57, 63, 65, 66, 68, 73, 75, 76, 78, and 86 were taken at three National Trust properties in the West Country — Cotehele on the River Tamar, Lanhydrock, near Bodmin and Saltram, Plymouth, to the staff of which we offer our special thanks.

The Potato Marketing Board would also like to thank the following companies for the loan of accessories for photography: *Royal Worcester · Boots Cookshop · Steelite T.G. Green · Harrods · David Mellor.*

Home Economists:
Suzanne Howe
Victoria Anthony
Gillian Gledhill

Food Photography:
David Warne

Design:
Wayne Boughen

Production/Editor:
Philip Boughen

Printing:
The Bracknell Press